The Chap Almanac

An Esoterick Yearbook for the Decadent Gentleman

Gustav Temple & Vic Darkwood

4th Estate   London

First published in Great Britain in 2002 by Fourth Estate. A Division of HarperCollins Publishers
77–85 Fulham Palace Road, London W6 8JB. www.4thestate.com

A catalogue record for this book is available from the British Library.   ISBN: 0-00-714643-4

Designed by M2, London. Printed by the Bath Press Ltd., Bath.

Introduction

Since the dawn of time, man has been engaged in a ceaseless quest to fathom the mystery of his destiny. He has looked to the galaxies for a blueprint of the human spirit; he has sought enlightenment through imitating the posture of the grasshopper; he has consulted priests, shamans and soothsayers, and he has even summoned hobgoblins from the depths of Hades to request advice, yet he is still none the wiser.

And what of the gentleman? With a natural abhorrence of all things 'alternative' or 'New Age' and a horror of any activity that involves sandals, loose clothing or penitence, how is he to quench his natural thirst for mystical truth?

Since the publication of The Chap Manifesto, reports began to trickle in from around the world that hinted at an answer to our queries. In regions as far-flung as Japan, Bolivia and Croydon, the threefold principles of grooming, etiquette and common courtesy that we hold dear seemed to be taking root. Nurtured by the singularities of the region they had sprung up in, these small pockets of Chappism were developing their own distinctive flavour, much like the joyous wines that can result when pinot grapes are cultivated in Chile.

We are now the curators of a towering personal library of manuscripts, leaflets, university papers and manuals, all of which chronicle some distant strand of Chappism. The logbook from a legendary voyage of discovery to Milton Keynes, for example, was kindly donated by one of the porters from the expedition. Members of Chappist cults such as the Temple of Morpheus and Aye Oh Yoo have sent us their Scriptures. We have also received countless newspaper clippings showing a clear Chappist influence on activities as unlikely as DIY, gardening, pet care, giving birth and military conflict.

It seems that every day of the year, somewhere in this magnificent orb, there is a fellow performing some ritual in accordance with the Chappist credo. The Almanac, that most ancient and civilized compendium of facts, festivals and forecasts, presented itself as the ideal form in which to bind our collection of esoteric curiosities. Thus the gentleman looking for an appropriate pastime to fritter away an afternoon, the layman in search of his inner dandy, or the lady whose beau is a dash on the shallow side – all will find within The Chap Almanac the spiritual guidance they seek.

Gustav Temple & Vic Darkwood

January
MORPHEUS

8: Sweet Intoxication. 11: *Pipe of the Month:* The Hookah. 12: Marcel Proust. 14: Pyjama Dharma.

 ### February
LIBIDO

20: The Art of Good Husbandry. 23: *Hat of the Month:* The Beret. 24: Femology. 28: Lady Hester Stanhope.

 ### March
SARTORIUS

32: Practical Uses for Pets. 35: *Pipe of the Month:* The Calabash. 36: Tie Kwon Do. 38: The Semiotics of Footwear. 41: Birth Patrol.

 ### April
EQUUS

44: Umbrella Jousting. 47: *Hat of the Month:* The Trilby. 48: Kenneth Gandar-Dower. 50: Betting Form. 52: Management Occultancy.

 ### May
THESAURUS

56: May Rituals. 58: Haughty Culture. 61: *Pipe of the Month:* The Churchwarden. 62: William Beckford.

 ### June
EPICURUS

66: Pater Divining. 69: *Hat of the Month:* The Boater. 70: The Brothers of Perpetual Indulgence. 74: Portion Control.

Morpheus

The dreamer, who greets the dawn of a new year in an opium-fuelled reverie

18th January 1904… Birthday Of Cary Grant in Bristol. As well as being a suave and dapper fellow, he was a keen user of LSD.

Sweet Intoxication

Dragging oneself away from the caress of one's perfumed sheets, rising and shining and facing the coming day with equanimity can be a pretty gruelling affair at the best of times, but confronted by the sub-zero temperatures of early January and the appaling prospect of a new year rolling out ahead of you, a fellow would justifiably feel inclined to roll over and sleep well into March. All this seems natural enough, but sooner or later a burgeoning bladder, cramp or bed sores will compel a fellow to venture out into the daylight and grasp the nettle with both hands.

Fully blown consciousness is not a happy state, even when negotiated with the aid of a brocade dressing gown, a head full of poetry and the fire of Dionysus in your soul. That is why, as any gentleman knows, no period of 24 hours should ever be embarked upon without at least a moderate consumption of narcotics. The only questions that face any man about town are what to consume, when and how to consume it, and how to accomplish this with verve, dignity and style.

By the term 'narcotics' we, of course, do not refer to the vulgar experimentation of so-called 'youth' who tend to take God knows what dubious concoctions to conjure God knows what dubious results. Designer drugs such as 'ecstasy' are rumoured to render one dance-crazed, enthusiastic and unnecessarily affectionate towards one's fellow man. It is frankly impossible to imagine anything worse.

The same goes for that drug of choice of the nouveau riche – cocaine. Self-satisfied media-types and ambitious city dealers on the razzle consume bucket-loads of this stuff in the hope that it will render them thrusting, dynamic and entertaining to the ladies. It has no place in the repertoire of the aesthete who, by his very nature, is born to sloth and inertia. The purpose of any narcotic (as the name implies, being derived from the Greek word, narke, meaning torpor) is to send a man's brain into languid contemplation and open the doors of perception to the mysterious vistas of the Infinite. Any drug that cannot be consumed profitably in the confines of a leather-upholstered armchair or clutched in a lady's heavenly embrace is, quite frankly, not worth the effort.

It becomes clear that intoxication must be regarded as a career for life rather than a weekend diversion. The following sections outline the mind-altering substances that a modern gent should consider sampling and the various effects he can expect to achieve.

Laudanum – Popularised by Thomas de Quincey's *Confessions of an English Opium Eater*, laudanum is the drug of choice for the decadent fop with absolutely nowhere to be in a

Fig. 1.

hurry. A few drops of this rosy-red tincture of opium deposited into a chilled glass of Chablis will start the day off as you mean to continue: flat out on your back, swooning in reverie. It should be noted, however, that long-term overuse of laudanum has the potential of playing merry hell with one's dress sense and eating habits. Opium must never be allowed to take precedence over a fellow's sartorial and gastronomic sensibilities.

The Dry Martini – On work days, when complete incapacitation might not seem the wisest course of action, greet the morning with a stiff martini cocktail. This highly invigorating concoction is a particularly efficient way to numb the mind to the horrors of public transport and paid employment. A thermos flask secreted under your desk will provide you with the stimulus you need to negotiate even the trickiest of office politics.

Snuff – The workplace is also an ideal environment in which to build up an impressive snuff addiction. Snuff comes in an agreeable range of varieties and can give one a powerful nicotine high whilst at the same time remaining nasally inoffensive to fellow staff. In an age where wrong-headed authority has declared most office areas 'smoke free zones', snuff provides the inveterate smoker with an essential life-line in a hostile environment.

The Tears of a Lady – Surely there are few substances more intoxicating to a gentleman than the tears of a lady. The next time your paramour sheds a tear or two due to your immoderate gambling habits, gather up her saline deposits in a handkerchief (Fig. 1) and inhale them with gusto. You will find yourself transported to pinnacles of untold delight.

Tea – Sometimes outshone by its more aggressively narcotic bedfellows, tea is one of the most subtle of all drugs. Highly refreshing and gently stimulating, regular cups of Lapsang

Souchong provide the body with a daylong subtle background level of toxins. In short, it is the very stage upon which the individual performances of stronger substances takes place.

Hasheesh – Thankfully, most right-thinking people avoid the realm of wage-slavery at all costs. This frees up considerable amounts of time for sitting around taking mind-boggling quantities of narcotics. A pungent hasheesh consumed using an Arabian hookah is a pleasant way of dispatching the wearisome hours of the afternoon (*see* Pipe of the Month). Invite your Moroccan friends around and don't worry if you don't speak a common language. Hasheesh may open the doors of perception, but robs its taker of the ability to articulate anything of any worth.

Old Books – Try grinding up the brittle pages of a rare 19th-century volume of the poems by Arthur Rimbaud in a mortar and pestle. Book collectors may blanche at this suggestion, but any bibliophile worth his salt will always have duplicate copies of his favourite books and destroying one will only add to the rarity value of the other. Such unnecessary vandalism will also add a *frisson* associated with the consumption of forbidden fruit. There is nothing that can quite compare to the decadent nasal sting produced by snorting a few carefully selected pages from *Une Saison en Enfer*.

Religious Relics – For an added twist on the previous section, the practice of grinding up and snorting religious relics is also calculated to send one's brain into paroxysms of spiritual ecstasy. In Spain and Italy, the reliquaries of obscure saints can be purchased at a snip. Imagine the thrill as half a gramme of pure San Valeriano's femur goes hurtling up your nostrils.

Chasing the Thurible – Scampering about the aisle during the progress of a religious service is not a very dignified or respectable practice, but a thurible billowing out heady clouds of frankincence can have a mesmerising effect on a fellow susceptible to perfume and transcendentalism. Getting close enough to gulp down one decent inhalation should have you walking on clouds for the rest of the day.

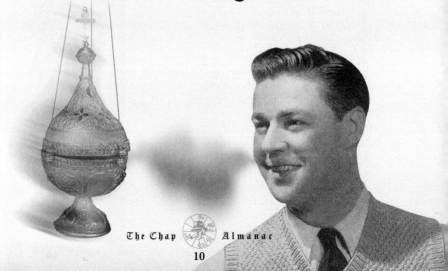

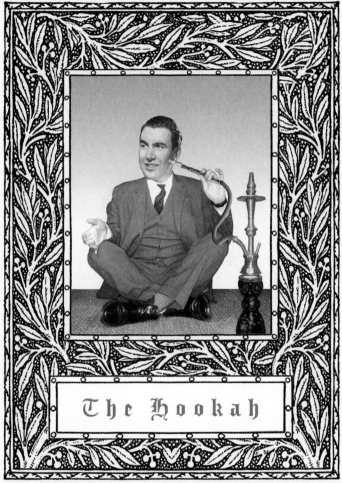

The Hookah

The inaugural weeks of a new year are renowned for their ability to send a sensitive soul tumbling into a morass of hopelessness and despair. Luckily, Madame Nature provides a jolly assortment of medicinal herbs for the treatment of such maladies. The services of a fine Arabian hookah have traditionally been employed as an invaluable pick-me-up for those wishing to bypass the worst excesses of the winter doldrums.

Marcel Proust

n 1st January 1909, Marcel Proust was reading in bed when he dipped a piece of toast into a glass of tea and remembered something he'd left behind in his childhood. Thus began a vast literary project that would run to a million and a quarter words and occupy the inert author until the day he died. Proust had discovered a novel way of accessing 39 years' worth of memories and converting them into fiction, so there wasn't much need for him to do anything else. Why run about creating new memories, when the old ones are simply stored away conveniently in the subconscious? It was simply a matter of retrieving them, and all one needed was time. Proust lost no time in converting his bedroom at 102 Boulevard Haussmann, Paris, into a hive of inactivity, remaining in bed for the next 12 years to write *Remembrance of Things Past*.

Proust's constitution was practically tailor-made for a lifetime in bed. His chronic asthma was so severe that only during the night could he breathe without frequent coughing fits. He developed a routine that involved getting up at five in the evening, writing all night, then retiring at dawn. With a single daily meal of one chicken wing, two eggs, three croissants, some chips, a bottle of beer and some coffee, his digestion was equivocal, requiring extensive laxatives every couple of weeks. He was unable to sleep unless girded by very tight underpants, which had to be fastened with a special pin. Insomnia plagued him throughout his life, and the insomniac often seeks solace in the very place where sleep is denied – in bed.

Illness defined Proust and lay him open to charges of hypochondria, but he was not without sympathisers. A legendary meeting between Proust and James Joyce began with someone asking Joyce whether he had read anything of Proust's. He remarked that, yes, he had read one of his sentences. When the meeting occurred, friends gathered around to eavesdrop on what would surely be a remarkable conversation. They were disappointed to hear the two literary giants discussing the effects of certain cheeses on their digestive systems.

But being an invalid confined to your bed can have its advantages, particularly for the novelist. Proust's isolation in his bedchamber heightened his senses, sometimes to intolerable extremes. He claimed to be able to sniff the perfume of someone standing two rooms away, and he'd have a quick asthma attack to confirm it. He had an understandable intimacy with his chamber pot, due to the risks involved in visiting the unhealthy chill of the lavatory. He would intentionally dine on asparagus, just to savour the pungent aroma of his urine wafting from the chamber pot below the bed.

Marcel Proust

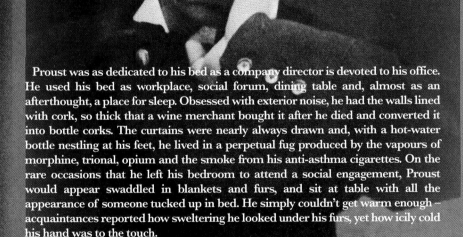

Proust was as dedicated to his bed as a company director is devoted to his office. He used his bed as workplace, social forum, dining table and, almost as an afterthought, a place for sleep. Obsessed with exterior noise, he had the walls lined with cork, so thick that a wine merchant bought it after he died and converted it into bottle corks. The curtains were nearly always drawn and, with a hot-water bottle nestling at his feet, he lived in a perpetual fug produced by the vapours of morphine, trional, opium and the smoke from his anti-asthma cigarettes. On the rare occasions that he left his bedroom to attend a social engagement, Proust would appear swaddled in blankets and furs, and sit at table with all the appearance of someone tucked up in bed. He simply couldn't get warm enough – acquaintances reported how sweltering he looked under his furs, yet how icily cold his hand was to the touch.

Proust completed his novel within hours of his death on 18th November 1922. He sent out for iced beer from the Ritz and drank it while giving instructions for the editing of his novel. When he finally gave up the ghost, the windows of the room were opened for the first time in 12 years as mourners filed in to pay their respects. Jean Cocteau, one of the visitors, said that the pile of manuscripts on the bedside table *"continues to live, like the ticking watch on the wrist of a dead soldier."*

Pyjama Dharma

As the sun rises over the snowy mountains of Tibet, the Buddhist temples dotted hither and thither are hives of activity. Monks are roused from their thin straw mats on the hard wooden floors and handed brooms, brushes and rakes while still half asleep. For the next two hours they must give their temple a thorough scrubbing, after which they receive a small bowl of boiled vegetables for breakfast. Thus begins a seemingly endless day of backbreaking meditation sessions, hours of toil in a freezing garden and some rather uninspiring chanting in the evening. The novitiate's reward for all this is a brief audience with the Master, who merely gives him a ludicrous conundrum to contemplate.

But in one exceptional temple the morning's ritual is altogether different. At dawn, the Master tiptoes into the dormitory, picking his way through discarded dressing gowns, hot-water bottles, half finished cups of Ovaltine, opium pipes and hookahs. The large four-poster beds emit the tranquil snores and heavy breaths of the sleeping acolytes. The Master bears a tray laden with small glasses of cognac laced with a few drops of laudanum. He gently awakens each monk in turn, hands him a glass and watches him drain its contents, before tucking him under the covers and moving on to the next bed.

These monks are in the second stage of their initiation period. Having retired at 9pm the previous evening, they are given a small aid at dawn to ensure they remain fast asleep until at least midday. For this is the Temple of Morpheus, the branch of Buddhism dedicated to sleep, dreams and lethargy.

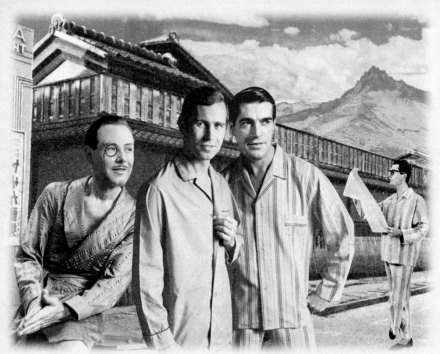

The Temple of Morpheus was founded in the early 19th century by Mikimoto Dozi, a lazy, good-for-nothing Japanese monk who had entered a Buddhist temple in the belief that he was opting for an easy life. But the reality of Buddhism was extremely unenlightening, most of its rituals being based on discipline, toil, meditation and fiddly crafts like calligraphy. Added to the 5am alarm call, the religion seemed specifically designed to exclude the easygoing, the languid and the plain bone idle.

It was when Dozi chanced upon the poem *Endymion* by John Keats that he realised his true calling. Endymion is a beautiful youth whom the gods grant eternal sleep so he can remain forever young. Dozi woke up from a secret afternoon nap in the temple with the sudden realisation that the path to true enlightenment lay not in relentless toil and sitting on straw mats all day, but in sleep and dreams. Dozi deserted his Buddhist temple, went straight to his hometown of Tokyo and bought several pairs of winceyette pyjamas, concocted some hot chocolate recipes, and returned to the hills of Tibet to found the Temple of Morpheus.

Dozi devoted seven years alone in a cabin founding the sevenfold path to Divana – enlightenment through sleep. It took him only a few actual weeks to create the doctrine, but Dozi devoted most of his seven years to monumental snoozes, occasionally poking an arm from under the heavy blankets of his four-poster to scribble a line or two of his sutra.

O for some drowsy Morphean Amulet!

The Sutra, or sacred text, of the Temple concerns itself with Morpheus, the god of dreams. Morpheus is the supreme ruler of the universe and the bringer of all that is good in the world. His opposite number is the evil Bransonia, dark lord of industry, exertion and wakefulness. In the Sutra of Morpheus, one of the many bedtime tales tells the story of Pyjama Dharma (tr. 'Truth of Sleep'), the battle between Morpheus and Bransonia over a game of tiddlywinks. Bransonia gets so distracted from the game by trying to reinvent it, sending faxes to his countless think-tanks and focus groups, that Morpheus, maintaining his concentration by taking light naps between every turn, easily wins the game.

The beliefs of the Temple of Morpheus also include reincarnation. It is written that if you devote yourself to the principles of the Temple, you will return in the next life as a dormouse (which spends two-thirds of its life fast asleep) or a three-fingered sloth. A monk who abandons Morpheus will come back in another life as a high-powered executive who sleeps three hours a night or, worse still, as an Olympic athlete.

Once novitiates have passed the initiation stage, they take their vows to enter upon the sevenfold path to Divana. This is as follows.

1. The path of true wisdom is best undertaken in a horizontal position.

2. The sleeping toad remembers what the leaping frog forgets.

3. We know the sound of one hand clapping, but what is the sound of one man napping?

4. He who is too tired to do something has found an excellent reason to take forty winks.

5. Exertion in dreams cannot offend the body; actual exertion can.

6. The natural spirit of man is clothed in winceyette pyjamas.

7. Being ready for bed is the noblest state to which man may aspire.

Upon initiation at the Temple, novitiate monks must renounce their daywear and are given two pairs of winceyette pyjamas, a silk dressing gown for summer and a woollen one for winter, and several pairs of monogrammed slippers. They are expected to give up all stimulants, such as coffee, coca-cola and newspapers.

During the first stage of initiation, novitiates receive instruction in the arts of composing bedtime stories, the filling of the hot-water bottle and the Ovaltine ceremony. They are trained to sleep for at least 12 hours a night as well as several snoozes throughout the day. With enough practice, monks should be able to nod off at any given time, even while standing under a tree. Dozi is said to be able to fall into a deep sleep even while jaywalking across a busy street in Tokyo.

The Temple of Morpheus is open to all. Monks have entered the order from every corner of the globe, and many monks have broken away from nearby Buddhist temples

where they have found the discipline unsuited to their lethargic temperaments. Unlike other temples, Morpheus also admits female monks. This has given rise to a few rumours over the years, with one scandal in the 60s that threatened the continuation of the Temple.

The rumours concerned afternoon group sessions with Dozi, known as 'the collective dream'. Dozi would begin by giving an interminably long speech (for which he consulted Fidel Castro of Cuba), causing all the monks to nod off in the comfortable armchairs of the lecture hall.

Once they were all asleep, Dozi would visit the monks in their dreams by astrally projecting himself into their subconscious. He is said to be able to control the dreams of

the monks by guiding their id by the hand – often into regions of the subconscious they may not be prepared to enter. Some of the female monks complained of waking up after a collective dream session feeling 'psychically interfered with'. One such female monk accused Dozi of leading her into his own dream, which happened to involve a sheer negligee, a pillow fight and a tub of chocolate mousse. Dozi responded to the accusation with a chuckle, saying, "In your dreams, baby!"

But the Temple of Morpheus has weathered the storm of mild controversy and continues to thrive to this day, with over 453 monks. With today's highly uninteresting lifestyles, and the furious pace at which we are expected to live them, more and more people are turning to Morpheus as a route towards a more spiritual existence. There is even a branch of the Temple in England, in the north of Shropshire, which has been flooded with applications since it opened in June last year. The staff of local shops have reported serving dreamy customers in pyjamas and dressing gowns. Sales of Ovaltine have never been so good.

Libido

The fellow who devotes the entire month to gaining access
to the hallowed Courts of Venus

The Art of Good Husbandry

St Valentine's Day has always been a good opportunity to give vent to Cupid's urges. The general presence of flowers and chocolates wafting through the streets puts a little pep and ginger into a man's footfall, imbuing him with the requisite valour to march up to a lady and request the pleasure of her company on the grand voyage that is marriage. It is worth bearing in mind, however, that the sophisticated lady of today has made a few alterations to her shopping list when it comes to looking for Mr Right. Gone are the days when the weary worker could return to his coop for an evening of dry martinis, freshly laundered shirts and a hearty meal, followed by a vigorous bout of canoodling with a pretty and willing wifelet.

It appears that while we gentlemen have been busy perfecting our cigarette lighting techniques and conducting amusing experiments with hair lacquer, the ladies have not been as quiescent as we perhaps imagined. Many of them have found cause to suspect that they too are entitled to a life of sitting at a desk for eight hours, in between three gruelling hours of commuting, relieved only by the occasional opportunity to bark orders at some subordinate. The resulting state of affairs resembles something of a volte-face within the marital home of today.

Most of today's ladies have jobs; of this we can be sure. These are a far cry from the feminine tasks of yesteryear, such as polishing bombs or cleaning aeroplanes. Today's professional lady can command six-figure salaries and some even have their own offices. To the staunch gentleman of leisure, this situation can be of more benefit than it sounds. Within the bond of Holy Matrimony, we will be permitted to spend the entire day abandoning ourselves to the muse (while the muse herself goes out and earns a crust), giving full vent to the artistic creations that well within us like a dormant Vesuvius.

Do not, however, allow yourself to get too carried away. As the day draws to a close, you can expect your beloved to arrive home after a hard day on mammon's exercise wheel and it is at this juncture that you must lay your notebook/harpsichord/tapestry aside and devote your attentions to her comfort. Here is a step-by-step guide to maintaining a happy, modern marital home.

1. First of all, prepare yourself for Mrs Chap's homecoming. Refresh yourself, wash off any stains you may have incurred during the day, and perhaps put a clean tie on. Be a little gay and interesting to your wife, for she will have spent the entire day with dull, ambitious people. Take her mind away from office politics by reading her a fragment of verse, plucking her a song on your lyre or by dancing a merry jig around her as she tries to barge past you into the nuptial home with her bulging briefcase.

2. Have a large, stiff drink ready as soon as Mrs Chap walks through the door. Take large draughts of it as you listen raptly to her account of her day. Perhaps even offer her a drink herself, if she feels like one. Many women are quite hungry when arriving home from work, so this might be a good time to enquire about dinner. If your wife's proposed menu is to your satisfaction, then you might want to help her put the apron on. If it is not, then this would be a good time to begin perusing the drawerful of takeaway menus in the kitchen.

3. Over dinner, speak in a low and soothing voice and listen carefully to your wife's conversation. Let her speak first, for her topics of conversation are much more important than yours. Remember, she is the mistress of the house and will ultimately be responsible for the utility bills and so forth, so it is probably best to keep on the right side of her. As soon as the meal is over, offer to make an appraisal of the evening's televisual offerings while she washes the dishes. This will give her a sense of being cared for and nurtured.

4. Never complain if your wife comes home late or extremely drunk. This is normal in the world of business and probably means she will soon be up for promotion – which is good news for you in the long run. Even if she neglects to come home at all until the following day, looking tired and dishevelled, count this as a positive benefit for the future of the household, and expect a few generous gifts over the next few days.

5. The key to enjoying the few shared hours you have together, as a result of Mrs Chap's professional commitments, is to include her in every activity – even the ones you would normally consider out of bounds for the ladies. For example, when you settle down on your Turkish cushions with the nozzle of your hookah firmly set between your teeth, you might ask Mrs Chap to read you a bedtime story, perhaps by Horace Walpole or John Polidori. As the Lebanese hashish takes its effect, your wife will gaze at you affectionately and plump up the cushions around your head, feeling that her long day at the office was all worth it.

6. When it comes to bedtime, your wife will need several minutes in the bathroom to lovelify herself for the boudoir. Make this easier for her by not making her wait too long outside the bathroom while you apply your hair net and de-wax your moustache. As every gentleman knows, these nocturnal grooming procedures can take up to an hour, so reward your wife for her patience by planting a mouthwash-enlivened kiss on her forehead as you relinquish the bathroom.

7. When it comes to intimate relations with your wife, it is important to remember that the modern lady has quite radical views on this matter. In all aspects of conjugal unpleasantness, be led by her wishes and wait for her to make the first move. If you're lucky, she will simply fall asleep as soon as she gets into bed, and you can settle back into a pleasant eight hours in the arms of Morpheus. Should your wife suggest congress, then accede humbly, being mindful that the woman's satisfaction is more important than the man's. When she reaches her moment of fulfilment, a small moan from yourself is encouraging, and quite sufficient to indicate any enjoyment you may have had. Should your wife suggest any of the more unusual sexual practices, get out of bed and give her a brief illustrated lecture on the dangers of syphilis and gonorrhoea. It is likely that your wife will fall promptly asleep immediately after lovemaking. This would be a good time to set the alarm clock for her, and put on a sturdy pair of earmuffs so it doesn't wake you up in the morning.

8. Preparations for the morning's breakfast should ideally be made the night before. This means that your wife will not have to be doing with such things first thing in the morning. When you arise, some four hours after she has left for the office, it makes a pleasant start to the afternoon to find a tray in the kitchen with teapot, cup, saucer, jug of milk, and a casserole full of fresh kedgeree in the oven.

The Beret

 As the sap begins to rise, making its steady journey from insole to nether region, a fellow's mind naturally turns to thoughts of love. However, impressionable ladies should certainly avoid wearers of that shapeless sack, known as the beret, that has long been the bastion of unsavoury continental types hellbent on sexual extremism. God knows what unspeakable code of ethics propels this fellow on his sickly journey of gallic excess.

Femology

To a chap-about-town, innocently going about his business, the inscrutable ways of the ladies are just about as impenetrable as the forces that govern the movements of the tides and the orbits of the celestial spheres. Generally inclined towards nuance and intrigue, ladies are genetically programmed to communicate with one another in ways virtually imperceptible to the male eye. They read 'atmospheres' as readily and as easily as we might read and understand the racing pages, the spatial possibilities of the billiard table or the metaphysical implications of French arthouse cinema. A lady may say one thing, but quite unbeknown to you or I, will mean something entirely different.

How many times, for example, have you attended an intimate supper with friends, only to find that when your guests have left, your ladylove has picked up an 'atmosphere' which she will describe as 'obvious', but, to you, registered precisely zero on the emotional Richter scale? "Cynthia is deeply unhappy," she will say. "Her hostility towards Derek was palpable." To which you will reply, "Nonsense, my dear, you're imagining things. The ideas you get into your silly little head!" Three days later, you read in the local newspaper that Derek has been found bludgeoned to death with a rolling pin, and you realise that your ladylove may have had a point after all.

On how many occasions has a lady assured you that her interest in you is entirely platonic, that your shared appreciation of the early compositions of Val Doonican is all that she requires for her lasting happiness, only to find a few hours later that she has transmogrified into an insatiable harpy, out for God knows what unspeakable pleasures?

How often, after a brief spell of frostiness with your *amoureux* amounting to no more than two or three hours, do you discover that in actual fact you are supposed to know 'what all of this is about' and, apparently, your liaison has been heading on a downward spiralling trajectory for the last two years?

Although the male may be biologically handicapped in the detection of 'atmosphere', there are a number of no-nonsense steps that a gent may take in furtherance of his understanding of the female gender. It seems that what the ladies refer to as 'atmosphere' may be less based on some mysterious extra-sensory perception and more on the acute observation of the subtleties of cranial structure and facial expression. A Chap hoping to gain insight into the inner workings of his ladyfriend's mind could do a lot worse than study the revelations that have been recently provided by the breathtakingly accurate science of Femology. The following pages summarise recent advances in what is likely to be a Nobel winning science.

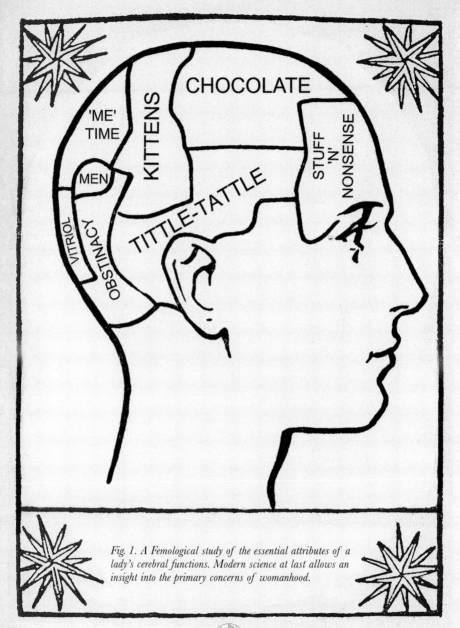

Fig. 1. A Femological study of the essential attributes of a lady's cerebral functions. Modern science at last allows an insight into the primary concerns of womanhood.

The Pout

It can sometimes be difficult to distinguish between the facial expressions that a lady reserves for her lover and her offspring. The Pout is a case in point. Before pregnancy, it is an incitement to sexual intimacy, but afterwards acts as a strong deterrent.

The Ingénue

Heavens, this poor creature looks as if she's in imminent danger of catching her death of cold. It can only be concluded that her innocent, childlike visage is a signal of pronounced learning difficulties, leading to absent-mindedness when dressing.

The Steely Gaze

Disconcerting and highly prevalent among truthseekers, such as customs officials, tax investigators and wives, the Steely Gaze is best dealt with by seeking refuge underneath nearby furniture or behind conveniently located walls or sofas.

The Impassive Aggressive

A single, quizzically raised eyebrow, combined with a look of the utmost composure, is enough to strike fear into any man's soul. Usually used by a disenchanted lady friend whilst in polite company as a chilling prelude to the storm that is yet to come.

THE FROWN

The attractively furrowed brow of a girl of impeccable breeding is often used to denote an exasperated lack of understanding of the ways of men. Any nonsense of this sort should be greeted with a firm but fair, "But that is the way of the world, my dear."

THE BOVINE

This jilted paramour demeans herself by making cow-eyes and dilating her nasal fittings to the point of unpleasantness. A woman's nostrils are very much akin to a classic pair of gentleman's trousers. On no account should they ever be flared.

THE AWESTRUCK

Sexual naivety in a newlywed bride may be regarded as a charming attribute. A fellow, on his wedding night, should not be surprised by a look of alarm upon his spouse's face. She is purely expressing dumbstruck wonderment at his manly nakedness.

THE HAUGHTY

This feisty minx is instinctively aware of her own worth. Although she may at first sight seem unobtainable, a hoity-toity demeanour is often a lady's way of asking to be stormed and overthrown like the discredited junta of a small South American republic. ◀

Lady Hester Stanhope

ⅎ **ew women can** have presented such a formidable challenge to the seasoned wooer than Lady Hester Stanhope. By the time Prince Pückler-Muskau arrived at her palace in Syria, this grand English aristocrat had established herself as the Queen of the Desert, ruling from an enormous seraglio on the pine-covered slopes of Deir Mashmoushe, southwest of Jezzine.

Lady Hester Stanhope had begun her life as a society hostess in Regency London. Her uncle was William Pitt, whose death in 1806 left his niece with a lifetime stipend from King George III. In 1810 she set off on a journey through the Middle East, accompanied by her long-suffering amanuensis, Dr Charles Meryon. She was the first European woman to enter the ruined citadel of Palmyra, being feted by its Bedouin denizens as a second Queen Zenobia, their ancient ruler.

By 1818, Lady Stanhope had settled permanently in Syria, initially as an honoured guest of the Emir Bashir II. As her influence grew over the local pashas, she gradually dispensed with all the formalities expected of foreign guests. She befriended the Emir's

relative and deadly enemy, Sheikh Beshyr, and curtly ceased all contact with the Emir, publicly denouncing his stupidity. This would have been worthy of execution in anyone else, but Lady Hester was viewed with a sort of supernatural awe by the Syrians and somehow exempt from punishment. She received many visitors at Djoun; Arabic dignitaries eager to curry favour with the 'Lady of Djoun', as she was known, as well as visiting Europeans come to pay their respects to the niece of William Pitt turned 'Europe's Mystery Lady of the Orient'.

One such cultural pilgrim was Prince Pückler-Muskau, a German princeling on a semi-permanent grand tour of the Orient. He took an immediate liking to her Ladyship, with whom he shared a disaffection with Europe. "Like you, my Lady," he wrote to her from nearby Sayda, "I look for future salvation from the East, where nations still nearer to God and to nature can alone, some day, purify the rotten civilisation of decrepit Europe, in which everything is artificial."

By then, Lady Stanhope was living in the 62-year-old shadow of her former glory. Her emaciated body was ravaged by frequent bleeding, pulmonary catarrh and complete lack of exercise. She had not left her palace at Djoun for four years, and was in the habit of rising between two and five in the afternoon and retiring at a similar hour of the morning. Conditions at the Stanhope household were by then woefully inadequate for a lady of her age and status. Extravagant building and gardening projects had saddled her with crippling debts, barely touched by her dwindling royal stipend. The brigands, thieves and layabouts she employed as servants routinely pilfered the lavish furnishings of her palace behind her back.

Prince Pückler-Muskau had a sense of humour and though genuinely interested in meeting the eccentric Lady of Djoun, he embarked upon a campaign of epistolary courtship as if wooing the greatest young beauty in all of Araby. Lady Stanhope had finally met an adversary who could match her in regal pomp and vanity. She always judged a man's breeding by the arch of his instep, inspecting the shape of her visitors' feet to assess their rank in relation to hers. She claimed her own instep was so high that a little kitten could run underneath it. Thus far, all her male visitors had proved sadly lacking in the shoe department. Of the French poet Lamartine, who visited her in 1832, Lady Stanhope said, "He thought to make a great effect when he was here, but he was grievously mistaken. Monsieur Lamartine pointed his toes in my face, then turned to his lapdog and held long conversations with him."

Prince Pückler-Muskau made a far greater impression. Her curiosity having been roused by the prince's daily letters, Lady Stanhope consulted his horoscope to find the most propitious day for their meeting. When the prince was informed of this date, he lied that he happened to be embarking on an expedition into the desert that day. His impertinence was rewarded with permission to visit at his own convenience.

Great preparations were made for the visit, with what little remained in the Stanhope household after years of plundering by the servants. The single rush-bottomed chair, deal table, two earthenware dishes and two silver spoons were made to look as agreeable as

possible. On Easter Monday, April 15th 1838, the prince rode into the courtyard, followed by his immense retinue and five mule-loads of baggage. He was dressed in an enormous Leghorn hat lined with green taffeta, a Turkish scarf over his shoulders and blue pantaloons of ample dimensions. The prince's most singular accoutrement was a tame chameleon that crawled about his pipe, to which he was as devoted as Lamartine had been to his lapdog. But Lady Hester was satisfied with her guest: the excellent fit of his tight Parisian boots revealed the thoroughness of his breeding.

The meeting was a success. The prince described Lady Stanhope as having the appearance of an ancient Sibyl, with pale, regular features, dark, fiery eyes, a sonorous voice and manners of Oriental dignity and calm. He stayed for a week, spending seven hours in lively and stimulating conversation with his hostess every evening. There was not much to eat, an oversight that Lady Stanhope explained by saying she lived like a dervish: "My roses are my jewels, the sun and moon my clocks, fruit and water my food and drink." She claimed that the Arabs viewed her not as man or woman, but as a being apart, an opinion she clearly shared with her adopted people.

The eccentric pair had common beliefs in astrology and demonology. Lady Hester was convinced of the glorious part she would play in the coming of a Messiah, or Mahedi, to Arabia. A local soothsayer had told her of an ancient book predicting the arrival of a European woman to live on Mount Lebanon, who would have greater power than the Sultan. The Mahedi would ride with her into Jerusalem on a horse 'born saddled'. Lady Stanhope firmly believed this reference was to her. In preparation, she kept two mares in her stable, one of which had a malformation on its back that resembled a saddle. The other was for the Lady of Djoun herself to ride alongside the Messiah on the great day.

The soothsayer had also predicted that the coming of the Mahedi would be preceded by great famine, pestilence and calamity. Sadly, this was the only part of the prophecy that came about during Lady Hester's lifetime. Her astronomical debts finally reached the attention of her royal benefactor, Lord Palmerston. He wrote informing that her stipend would be stopped unless she paid her debts, which then amounted to some £10,000.

Lady Hester responded with characteristic hauteur. On 12 February 1838, she wrote an ultimatum to the Queen, which was to be published in the British newspapers if ministers refused to show it to Her Majesty. She threatened to renounce her stipend if anyone suggested its termination, adding that she would wall herself up in her palace if her financial affairs were not put in order.

When she received no response from the Queen, she abandoned all hope of restoring her reputation. By then, Lady Stanhope was barely able to move her skeletal frame from the single, tattered sofa remaining in the house. From there, she directed her servants to carry out her final building instruction. They were to wall up the gates to the house, sealing off the palace entirely from the outside world. All the servants were dismissed, except for two maids and a boy. Lady Hester spent the last year of her life in this tomb-like seclusion, gradually wasting away until her death in June 1839.

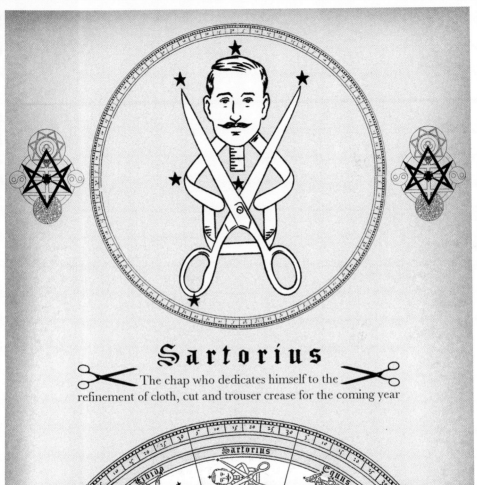

Sartorius

The chap who dedicates himself to the refinement of cloth, cut and trouser crease for the coming year

Practical Uses for Pets

𝔓 sychologists are yet to provide a convincing explanation as to why otherwise
rational human beings have a propensity to introduce a variety of ill-mannered
beasts into their homes, feed and pamper them, and refer to them as 'pets'. Pets are
almost as pointless and bloody-minded as children, and in most people's experience a
brood of the latter will almost certainly lead, at some point or other, to a brutish
menagerie of the former. Through God knows what genetic predisposition, the
Englishman is particularly prone to this sort of nonsense and we grudgingly have to
admit that at least some animals have the potential to add style to one's daily
proceedings. For instance, walking into a film premiere with a lady friend confidently
leading a diamond-collared puma is always apt to raise a few eyebrows, and a man who
can enliven a rather dull evening at the Ivy by producing a white pigeon from the dark
recesses of his suit sleeve will be roundly thanked by fellow diners. But generally
speaking, a house full of pets forms a menacing and disgruntled alliance hellbent on
making you feel outnumbered, guilty and a stranger in your own home.

So it comes as very good news indeed to learn that a new technique has been designed
to make both your life and the lives of your pets more tolerable. Loosely based on
current practice in zoological gardens, by which keepers maintain the contentment of
their wards by setting them various challenges (such as requiring polar bears to retrieve
their fishy suppers from a large plastic buoy, or encouraging rats and gerbils to track
down their food through a series of intricate mazes), a responsible pet owner can
instigate a *rapprochement* with his bestial entourage by making them feel valued and
usefully occupied.

Spring is a particularly suitable time to do this. Pets will be emerging from their winter
dormancy and the sap will be rising in their veins, making them restive and competitive
with each other, and a little testy with their owners. March is also regarded as a jolly
good juncture to do a spot of spring-cleaning, dusting things down and putting one's
household affairs in some semblance of order. It is a relatively simple matter to combine
concern for one's pet with the whole host of domestic duties that are are crying out to
be attendend to, providing valuable help for you and an enormous sense of wellbeing
for your pet.

Inspired by the above, any fellow of imagination should be able to conjure up at least a
dozen methods of keeping his pets happy. Here are but a few of those currently in vogue.

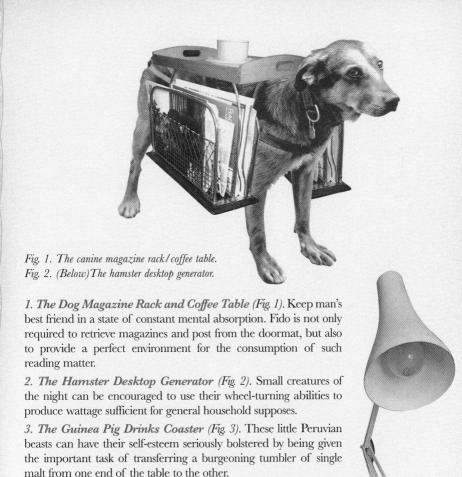

Fig. 1. The canine magazine rack/coffee table.
Fig. 2. (Below)The hamster desktop generator.

*1. **The Dog Magazine Rack and Coffee Table** (Fig. 1).* Keep man's best friend in a state of constant mental absorption. Fido is not only required to retrieve magazines and post from the doormat, but also to provide a perfect environment for the consumption of such reading matter.

*2. **The Hamster Desktop Generator** (Fig. 2).* Small creatures of the night can be encouraged to use their wheel-turning abilities to produce wattage sufficient for general household supposes.

*3. **The Guinea Pig Drinks Coaster** (Fig. 3).* These little Peruvian beasts can have their self-esteem seriously bolstered by being given the important task of transferring a burgeoning tumbler of single malt from one end of the table to the other.

The Chap Almanac

4. The Chinchilla Duster. Any soft-haired rodent worth its salt would give its eye-teeth to be involved in the stimulating task of household dust control. Clasp your chinchilla firmly about the abdomen and utilise the finer back-hair to buff up polished wooden surfaces.

5. The Phainopela Air Conditioning Unit *(Fig. 4)*. Exotic birds of many varieties may be efficiently exercised whilst providing much-needed ventilation on warm days through simple technology involving pencils and Sellotape.

Fig 3. (Above) The guinea pig drinks coaster.

6. Cat Racing. A rained-off meeting at Wincanton or Redcar will no longer spell betting disaster and feline runners will gain self-confidence from your lusty vocal encouragements.

It soon becomes evident that through the application of such simple remedies, household beasts, rather than spending their lives in an endless torment of unrealised potential, can gain satisfaction from knowing that they are making themselves useful to their masters and fulfilling their brutish destinies with stylishness and aplomb. In the final analysis, what could possibly give a humble animal more pleasure and satisfaction?

Fig. 4. Muggy days can be rendered far more tolerable with the aid of a pencil, an exotic bird and a roll of Sellotape.

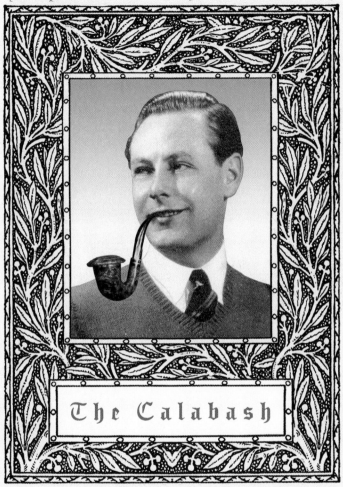

The Calabash

A fellow with a penchant for aestheticism and style will naturally opt for a smoking implement which reflects his obsessions. With eyes of blue crystal, the shimmering face of an angel and a penchant for all things beautiful, this aesthete reveals the true secret of his eternal youth only by his choice of smoking implement. The calabash might rightly be regarded as the serpentine conduit of Beelzebub.

Tie Kwon Do

Picture the scene: you are strolling along a city thoroughfare with your good lady wife, dressed immaculately in a bespoke serge two-piece suit from Henry Poole, a Harvie & Hudson ivory poplin shirt, a Liberty print tie and a pair of Cleverly legates. Suddenly, a particularly amusing bon mot you are delivering to your ladylove is interrupted by the arrival of a brigand of youths. From within the hooded tops of their tracksuits come imprecations for you to relinquish the contents of your wallet. Naturally, the only possible course of action is to engage the services of a passing police constable.

Unless, of course, you have been trained in the Sartorial Arts. This ancient system of self-defence has been practised in Southern China since the days of the Tang Dynasty. It was devised by Ching Mun, a journeyman tailor who based the system on a fight he witnessed in a field between a rat and a peacock. Ching Mun observed how easily the peacock overcame the rat, not through the use of brute strength, but by strutting about and showing off its dazzling plumage. The Academy of Ching Mun-Ho still flourishes today, training some 250 adepts every year in the techniques devised by its founder to overcome any form of physical attack purely by using tailoring skills.

THE SKIN OF THE COBRA

Once the adept has mastered basic tailoring skills, he will be put to work on lining a suit jacket with reflective silver material. When confronted by a brigand of poorly dressed ruffians, he simply flings open his jacket to them. The reflected glare will momentarily blind them, and once the scrofulous individuals catch the reflection of their shabby tracksuits, compared with the superb cut of their opponent's schmutter, they will hang their heads in shame and amble away in a state of sartorial ignominy.

TIE KWON DO

Many months at the Academy are devoted to the practice of knotting ties, with a total of 65 different recognised styles. An adept who has reached Black Tie status, the highest grade of knotmanship, will be able to garrotte an assailant by wrapping a tie around their throat in such a way as to entirely disable them. The knot he uses will be so complicated that even if the hold is relinquished, the assailant will not understand how to loosen the tie, thus rendering him vulnerable to further sartorial attacks.

The Eye of the Needle

There is an old tailoring technique known as the Rock of the Eye, which is the ability to judge the required cut of a suit merely by observing a client's physique without recourse to any awkward questions regarding 'which side Sir prefers to dress'. At Ching Mun-Ho, adepts are trained to hone this ability into a powerful weapon against their assailants. Once they have ascertained which side their attacker dresses on, they simply need to place a well-aimed kick to his testicular region, thus disempowering him long enough to make a run for it.

Bare Buttock Boxing

One of the simplest of the Sartorial Arts, yet the most difficult to master. The technique requires that, at the crucial moment – your timing must be precise within a millisecond – you whip out your calling card, upon which you have written the word 'sodeomite' (all the more effective if misspelled) and place it in his top pocket (if indeed he has one). This will enrage your opponent so much that he will rush off to formulate a new set of rules for boxing. But before the rules have time to be put into practice, you prod him sharply in the buttock with your umbrella and run away laughing.

The Daddy Long-Legs

Young people these days experience incredible difficulty in keeping up with changes in correct waistband levels. A bizarre form of one-upmanship now exists based on how ludicrously low-slung the trousers are worn. The skilled Sartorial Artist will exploit this by always wearing braces. When confronted by a low-waistbanded ruffian, he will swiftly elevate his own waistband to its maximum height by adjusting his braces. The resulting sight will momentarily confuse his assailants, who will enter into a heated discussion on current waistband fashions. The Sartorial Artist will choose this moment to make good his escape. ✂

30th March 2000… The Philippines' shoemaking capital of Marikina acquired 200 pairs of shoes from Imelda Marcos's 1200-strong collection for the Marikina City Footwear Museum.

The Semiotics of Footwear

It is common knowledge that 60% of a man's identity resides in his footwear. (A further 20% being made up by the brand of cigarette he smokes.) Whilst manners maketh man, it is his shoes that defineth him and quite literally give him standing in society.

Shoes in all their manifestations have a unique position in a gent's wardrobe of acting as the interface between his bodily person and the world on which he stands. They are the very foundation of a man's universe and reveal much about how he sees himself in relation to his surroundings. A man denuded of an appropriate pair of pedal appendages is no better than a floundering worm in a kingdom of millipedes.

Any appraisal of one's fellow man should therefore start with a brief glance down in the direction of God's good earth and the hoof attire he has selected to place upon it. This should give you virtually all the information you require to distinguish friend from foe, and abject knave from thoroughly decent fellow.

THE OXFORD

As eloquent as a letter of recommendation from the Marquis de Sade, the Oxford singles a man out as a fellow worth serious consideration. A foot clad in well-polished and immaculately-crafted leather acts as a passport to the realms of the sublime.

THE TRAINER

What vile barbarianism is afoot here? The perfidious ailments known as 'youth' and 'sport' can so damage a fellow's critical faculties that cladding one's feet in tawdry plastic and rubber presents itself as a perfectly reasonable dress option. It is not.

THE BROGUE

If Dionysus were to be incarnated as an Englishman he would undoubtedly favour the brogue as a fitting accompaniment to his robust lifestyle. Ideally suited to outdoor activities such as dashing about in Arcadian glades in hot pursuit of nymphs and dryads.

THE BROTHEL CREEPER

Favoured by crazed ragamuffins addicted to Thunderbird wine, duck's bottoms and rock 'n' roll, these crepe-soled absurdities are the calling-card of callow and virgin youth. A mature man attends his assignations at the bordello with certitude and pride.

THE LOAFER

Despite its promising name, the Loafer is chiefly the domain of hard-working middle-management who signify their leisure hours through the sickly cult of the tassel. A man skilled an the art of lassitude has no need of shoes that advertise the fact.

THE SANDAL

These flimsy artefacts may seem perfectly acceptable to antipodean back-packers, fundamentalist Christians and hirsute environmentalists, but in truth they are only suitable for wear in the hotter colonies. They certainly have no place north of Gibraltar.

THE SLIPPER

Languor is the badge of all right-thinking men, and slipper-usage (in conjunction with a brocade dressing gown) is a daily staple. They should not, however, be worn for dining – such a practice marks the wearer out as either bourgeois or dangerously eccentric.

THE WINKLE-PICKER

Though a trifle outré, this pointy-nosed creation can, if accompanied by acerbic wit, wads of cash and a 5000-acre estate in Hampshire, single its wearer out as a man of charming unconventionality and creative genius.

THE EXOTIQUE

The only acceptable mode of dress for a night in with one's hookah and friends from North Africa, this festive adornment takes up where the slipper leaves off. Especially effective in establishing one's decadent credentials when worn during business meetings.

THE OVER-DESIGNED

Concepts such as 'fashion' and 'designer labels' have no place in the wardrobe of a gentleman. A designer who claims to have 'reinvented the concept of the shoe' is a charlatan and singles his customers out as gullible or, even worse, nouveau riche.

30th March 2003… Mother's Day, when all decent gentlemen send their houseboys to the maternal nest with a dry martini and a single red rose.

Birth Patrol

Our libraries, bookshops and charity shops are awash with guides for the mother-to-be on what positions to adopt when her progeny is about to burst on to the scene, but what of the pater-in-waiting? Here is a suggested series of birthing positions calculated to make the transition from boulevardier to progenitor as painless as possible.

1. CONCEPTION

Having inseminated a willing lady, settle back against the pillows with an expression of smug contentment underscored with abject terror at the reality of what you have done.

2. CONFIRMATION

When the presence is confirmed in your collaborator's womb of a guaranteed drain on your paltry financial resources, lie back and think of Scotland with the help of a bottle of Glenfiddich.

The Chap Almanac

3. Morning Sickness

While your lady languishes in pre-natal classes, you will find yourself at a loose end. Your attempts to fill the endless hours constructively will inevitably end in failure. This is the most efficacious position to adopt after a particularly monumental failure the previous night.

4. Sweepstake

As the nine months come to an end, your chums will be eager to wager on the gender of the projected infant. Adopt an authoritative stance next to a small blackboard for this purpose.

6. Introductions

When presented to the little fellow or filly for the first time, affect a natural and casual air; in other words, let the blighter see you as you really are.

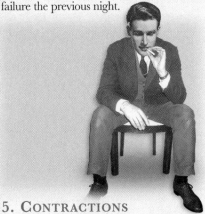

5. Contractions

When your lady begins to feel the unstoppable life force ready for exit, you will find yourself in hospital corridors for long periods. Build up your strength during pregnancy by raising your tolerance for nicotine, for there will be much smoking to be done while you wait.

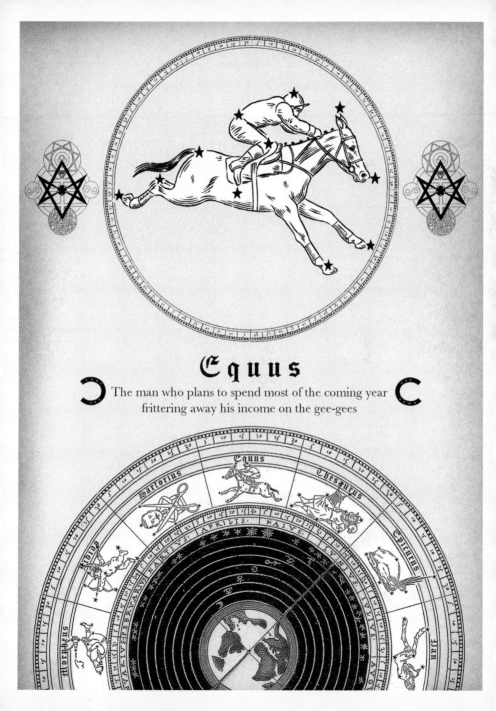

Equus

The man who plans to spend most of the coming year
frittering away his income on the gee-gees

April 23rd 1350… King Edward III founded the Knight's Order of St George of the Garter at Windsor Castle.

Umbrella Jousting

It is tremendously difficult in this day and age for a chap of mettle and valour to find an appropriate arena in which to put his manly qualities to the test. Traditionally, the more robust and pugilistic specimens of manhood have found themselves channelled by the education system into the dull-witted and unhealthy pursuit of sport, swiftly followed by an extended stint in the desperately rough domain known as 'the military'. All very well and good, but such an outdoor approach to martial conflict has a bad reputation for bagging-out the knees of one's legwear and ruffling a finely sculpted coiffure.

Luckily, history has provided us with a number of alternatives to bare-faced bellicosity. One of these is the chivalrous art of jousting.

To the urban dweller, jousting may seem like an inconsequential folk memory that occupies that small portion of grey matter dedicated to medieval pageants and half-remembered Hollywood epics. How on earth could massive shire horses, damsels in pointy hats and 15 hundredweight of metal plating have any relevance to contemporary living? But, necessity, we are constantly being reminded, is the mother of invention, and young urban males are currently adapting the elaborate code of medieval knighthood to fulfil the requirements of far more up-to-date concerns. Gone are the sturdy lances and heavy armoury, and in their place we find that ubiquitous piece of hardware, the rolled umbrella, and a classically-tailored three-piece worsted.

On the bustling thoroughfares of our great metropolises, a fellow's patience can often be tested to breaking point. Pushing and untold impudence from one's fellow man will lead one into unseemly fracas and heated verbal exchanges. No more is this true than on the platforms and escalators of railway and underground stations, where a blind determination to get from A to B plays merry hell with the gentler qualities of the human heart. In forays into the lower reaches of hell, currently renamed Tottenham Court Road tube station, you will find yourself under constant pressure to hold your own, mark out your territory and punish your fellow man for his stupidity, selfishness or olfactory offences against your perfumed nostrils.

Fig. 1.

For a young turk on the prowl a rolled umbrella now becomes a heraldic symbol of his code of chivalry. Nothing is calculated to make his blood boil more than espying a mobile phone user descending on an adjacent escalator (Fig. 1). It is time to harness the momentum of the moving staircase and to turn the contraption into an impromptu jousting pitch. Honour dictates that he should do his utmost to dislodge the offensive instrument from the hands of the user and, if possible, inflict a lengthy gash on his cheek. This will act as a warning to any foolhardy mobophiles wishing to repeat the offence.

Although umbrella jousting is ideally suited to spontaneous acts of chastisement for the wrong-headed, it only really comes into its own when two gentlemen of equal refinement and standing decide to pit themselves against each other. This might be for the love of a lady, to settle an argument over the relative merits of literary genres, to offset a pressing gambling debt or even for sheer devilment. When little is at stake 'Joust a Plaisir' (for pleasure) will be entered into, the victor being decided on the basis of points scored. In the advent of a more heinous grievance, a 'Joust à l'Outrance' (to the death) is likely. However, in this cossetted and namby-pamby age, the term 'to the death' is more a metaphor than an actuality, honour being satisfied by a heavy seepage of blood or the paltry loss of an

Fig. 2. Classic stances – To Arms, The Parry-Flounce, Le Petit Galop and The Lunge.

Fig. 3. 'Now gents, I want a good, clean fight'. Mohammed, a guard at Clapham Junction station, is happy to act as an impromptu umpire.

eye. For bouts 'a plaisir' the scoring system is relatively simple. One point for a glancing contact, two for a 'grand frappé' (a more substantial blow, possibly slightly disfiguring a nicely tailored lapel) and three for a 'grand frappé (recumbent)' in which a fellow finds himself unceremoniously flipped fundament over tip. It is left to the umpire's discretion to award extra points for the stylishly unseating of an opponent's hat or the fortuitous destruction of a mobile phone. Further bonus marks may be gained for the shininess of a contestant's shoes or the crease in his trousers.

Women are rumoured to find the spectacle of two healthy young men in mortal combat a most exhilarating experience, and the peacock prowess of umbrella jousting probably owes as much to the need to impress nubile ladies as it does to settling scores. Some of the stances are highly theatrical and show off a fellow's calves to immaculate perfection. Take, for example, the Parry-Flounce (Fig. 2), a typical piece of bravura in which a contestant saucily 'camps it up' whilst repelling his opponent's blows as a way of displaying complete nonchalance under attack. Or, possibly, the Cross-Parry (Rampant) where a jouster draws himself up to his full height to display unshakeable self-confidence.

For those wishing to experiment with the charms of umbrella jousting for the first time, one could do no better than visit Clapham Junction (Britain's busiest railway station) in South London. The sheer weight of commuter traffic will lead to numerous opportunities for a fellow to test his steel, and the long and numerous platforms provide ample space for a high speed tilting. The staff are courteous and are happy to act as an impromtu umpire when two enraged commuters prepare to clash (Fig. 3). After 45 minutes of stampeding across the asphalt you may arrive at your place of employment slightly scuffed and sanguinated, but when you look into the mirror that evening, the slightly paunchy, anaemic pen-pusher you once saw will have been transmogrified into a noble warrior – a Sir Galahad of the Suburbs. ◉

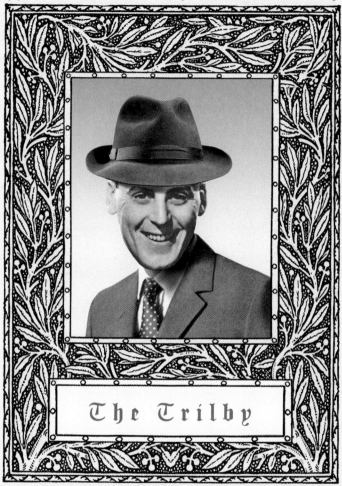

The Trilby

The traditional garb of the equine enthusiast, this craftily aerodynamic piece of hat construction allows its wearer to slip anonymously through the throng at race meetings, building up gargantuan gambling debts and relentlessly plying young ladies with choice snippets of Rabelaisian filth. A conventional appearance is very often the mask of a singularity of character or a soul mired in Hades.

Kenneth Gandar-Dower

Training greyhounds to chase a mechanical hare is no mean task; encouraging thoroughbred horses to bear the weight of a sinewy Irishman for three-and-a-quarter miles over fences is an even nobler vocation. But outranking them both for sheer bravado against all the odds is the desire to train cheetahs to race each other around dog tracks. Kenneth Gandar-Dower was a fellow with just such an ambition, which he miraculously fulfilled in 1937.

Kenneth Gandar-Dower distinguished himself at Harrow in the 20s by showing an aptitude for a multitude of sports, namely lawn tennis, squash, cricket, fives, bowls and billiards. His bowling got him selected for the school's second eleven against Winchester in 1927, and later his skills on the tennis court took him to the second round at Wimbledon. There is obviously nothing particularly impressive to a gentleman about sporting successes, unless they involve a pack of cards or a bookmaker, and it is Gandar-Dower's achievements on an altogether different set of fields that are worthy of our attention.

In August 1934, he made the first of many trips to Africa. He planned to scour the whole of Mount Kenya for a mythical beast he had called the Spotted Lion, of which there was no record in Europe. Arriving in Nairobi via the Suez Canal, Gandar-Dower's initial impression of the Dark Continent showed a clear anti-Globalisation stance: "Kenya was a greater blessing to the world when she produced imaginings and wonder rather than sisal and coffee."

Progress through the savannah was slow, due to incompetent porters and Gandar-Dower's lack of equine experience. He was also ill equipped for safari adventure, barely

able to handle a rifle and too emotional about killing wild prey. His first bagging of a lion sent him loopy with remorse, and he stripped naked and ran into the veldt to try and sympathise with the experience of a zebra being stalked by a lion. Gandar-Dower returned to England with nothing to show for his trip but a slim volume entitled *The Spotted Lion*, whose publication passed almost unnoticed in the newspapers.

Gandar-Dower made a second trip to Africa in 1935, this time with slightly more success, although not in locating spotted lions. He became the first European to capture a giant forest hog and produced the definitive map of the Sattima Mountain. But his prize catch was 12 cheetahs, which he brought back to England in December 1936. They had to remain in quarantine for six months, during which time Gandar-Dower built them a splendid set of living quarters at Croydon. His plan was to have the cheetahs race at greyhound tracks against dogs.

A marvellous idea, and one which would liven up many a bookmaker today, but there were some unforeseen contingencies. While greyhounds are happy to gather full speed in pursuit of an electronic hare, cheetahs need to smell flesh and blood before being roused into action. They also tend to work more effectively alone, as opposed to chasing prey in packs in the manner of the lion or the beagle. Another unforeseen result of transferring these speedy beasts from the open savannah to the circular dog track is that, although able to reach 70mph in a few seconds, they are not very skilled at rounding corners.

Gandar-Dower had his work cut out, but by then he was so possessed by the notion of racing these animals that he devoted all his considerable energies to it. He became very attached to his cheetahs and took to wandering around London with one of them on a lead. Members of his club were intrigued by his visits accompanied by this singular feline companion and the sport of cheetah racing looked set to gather plenty of punters.

Demonstrations were held at the White City stadium, where the cheetahs displayed remarkable speeds, if a little sketchy on the corners. Gandar-Dower was granted the use of Haringey Dog Track as a practice run for the cheetahs, and they began to run proper races in the evenings after the dog racing had finished.

Cheetah racing proved popular enough among the punters and money changed hands accordingly. The biggest threat to the public was the cheetahs' feral background; if they were able to rip a gazelle to shreds in a few minutes, what might they do to a portly fellow in a cloth cap, quietly grazing on a pie and a glass of stout?

In the end, it was not a savage mauling that turned the authorities off cheetah racing, but their inability to round the corners. At one of the trial races at Haringey, one of the speeding beasts came off a bend and knocked a punter flying into the stands. Gandar-Dower was denied his racing licence and forced to return his dozen cheetahs from whence they came.

Kenneth Gandar-Dower quite naturally turned his attentions to squash. He won the 1938 Bath Club Championship and went on to win for England against Scotland. After that, the Second World War broke out and he was blown up by a Japanese submarine in 1944. ◉

Betting Form

There is an unmistakable aura of secrecy and privilege about the high street bookmakers. Its imposing façade, shrouded with the arcane symbols of equine and canine tournaments, exudes a subtle air of *comme il faut*, as if the doors were firmly locked to the uninitiated and wide open to those in the know. It doesn't take a huge amount of study to learn the correct etiquette of betting shops, and the rewards can be of great benefit to both purse and self-esteem.

DRESS CODE

To the untrained eye, the clients of a betting shop might appear not to have dressed in any particular way at all – in short, they present a downright scrofulous aspect. Yet, closer inspection reveals that there are as many sartorial *sine qua nons* in a bookmaker's as there are at a formal dinner with the Prince of Wales. The desired look is charity shop chic with a hint of despair. A striped blue-and-white tie, for example, is twinned with a checked green cardigan and a pair of nylon trousers, rounded off with a fawn jacket with sagging pockets and a khaki pork pie hat.

HEIRACHY

The most important rule of conduct at the betting shop is to acknowledge the hierarchy of punditry and personnel. Each must be greeted appropriately, while certain genuflections are required for the higher-ranking members.

At the lowest level, but since you are a newcomer still your superior, is the construction worker on his lunch break. This rough-hewn fellow in paint-spattered overalls will only be on the premises for an hour but must always be addressed as 'Sir'. Next is the gaggle of chain-smoking Orientals. They are serious gamblers and generally keep themselves to themselves; any contact with them should be preceded by a discreet bow. You may notice a nervous looking City worker in the corner, clutching a copy of the Financial Times. This occasional punter and dilettante can be curtly ignored. The highest-ranking punter is the elderly Jamaican fellow, who must always be addressed as 'Your Excellency'. You must take great care never to obstruct his view of the racing screens, for he will have a wager on everything running, from the Catford Dogs to the number on the Richter scale of the next earthquake in Bolivia.

The cashiers should be addressed as 'My Lord' or 'My Lady'. Should you happen to catch a glimpse of the Turf Accountant himself behind the counter, a respectful doff of the hat is appropriate. If he should address you, which is highly unlikely, a brief comment on the weather will suffice, followed by 'Your Highness', but do not for an instant suppose that he is the least bit interested in your conversation.

Placing A Bet

Take a seat at one of the booths and approach each item on the table in front of you in the order shown in Figure 1. Working your way from the outside in, begin by lighting a cigarette and studying the form for the next race in the Racing Post. Take a swig of lager, fill in the betting slip and hand it with your wager to one of the cashiers.

Once the race begins, it is much better form to shout at the jockeys, whose names you must know, rather than the horses. Always defer to the highest-ranking punter; so if the elderly Jamaican is backing Misty Phroag in the 4.15 at Ludlow, then lend your vocal support to this nag, even if you haven't got a bet on it.

If your horse doesn't win, you must tear up your betting slip with a flourish, but only twice. Shredding the slip into tiny pieces and flinging it over everyone like confetti is generally frowned upon. It is conversely very bad form to acknowledge a victory. A deep inward sigh of relief is quite sufficient. Although upon your first visit to a bookmakers it may appear that nobody ever wins, this is not the case. As His Excellency will observe, if pressed on the point, "We're all winners here."

Fig. 1.

April 8th–10th, 1904… Aleister Crowley was dictated The Book of the Law by the god Horus in Cairo.

Management Occultancy

𝕭𝖑𝖆𝖈𝖐 𝕸𝖆𝖌𝖎𝖈𝖐 𝖘𝖔𝖑𝖚𝖙𝖎𝖔𝖓𝖘 𝖋𝖔𝖗 𝖆𝖓 𝖔𝖛𝖊𝖗-𝖊𝖋𝖋𝖎𝖈𝖎𝖊𝖓𝖙 𝖜𝖔𝖗𝖐𝖋𝖔𝖗𝖈𝖊

Fig. 1. The Master Magician, or Thoth, instructs a board of directors on the use of Magick Occultancy.

This somewhat alarming brochure, we found, reveals the extremes with which some members of the Chappist fold have applied our principles. However, needs must when the Devil drives, as they say, and who are we to stand in the way of anyone dedicated to furthering the Grand Cause?

Ahoy, Manager! Is your business staffed by a devoted team of project managers whose sole concerns are growth, profit and global positioning for your product? Is the only sound in your office the collective hum of rattling keyboards, flickering monitors and clicking mice – the electromagnetic throb of money being made? If the answer is yes, then by Lucifer, you need help.

Satanick Corporate Solutions™ will transform an efficient modern workforce using Black Magick. We are not the least bit impressed by such concepts as 'middleware business logic' and 'front-end user interfaces' – we are the servants of Beelzebub, Horus and Eblis and our only goal is pandemonium. Our highly trained team of magicians, witches and devil worshippers will use hypnotism and magick to repair the psychic damage inflicted on your staff by years of corporate abuse. We will convert your writhing Hydra of collective efficiency into a harmonious den of languor, bonhomie and *joie de vivre*. The root problem of an over-efficient workforce is always the same: the employees.

The first stage of our Great Work is to indentify the key members of staff who need maladjusting. They are usually defined as one of the following four types.

1. Goody Two-Shoes: He/she never takes a break of any description, not even to go to the lavatory. Any offers of tea, coffee and, particularly, alcoholic beverages are stoutly refused on the grounds that they will interrupt the flow of work. What is worse, Goody Two-Shoes makes everyone else feel guilty whenever they so much as stop working for a gulp of fresh air.

2. The Alpha Male: An aggressive go-getter who is always setting new targets for the company (which he ludicrously refers to as 'We') and expects everyone else in the office to take the whole wretched business of paid employment seriously.

3. Mr Headphones: The trendy person in the office who insists on coming to work dressed in the latest casual fashions, sneering at anyone who hasn't heard of his absurd labels. He always has a Walkman clamped to his ears, emitting the grating hiss of 'techno' music.

4. Captain Memo: Obsessively sends circular memos to announce meetings, followed by a meeting report. The meetings are frequently about such trifles as tidying the stationery cupboard. Yet when you try to engage him in casual conversation around the water-cooler, he rushes off to reply via email, circulated to the entire staff.

THE GREAT WORK

Here are some example spells to perform on the above-mentioned members of staff.

MR HEADPHONES

The first unpleasant characteristic to deal with is Mr Headphones' appalling dress sense. You must invoke Corby, Dark Lord of the pressed trouser. First, draw a pentagram on the floor with chalk. Place a Corby Trouser Press within the pentagram and recite the following Latin invocation.

"Benedictus Corbus Pantalonus Pressum
Terminus dictatoriat Levi Strauss oficinus Sartorius!"

Recite this as you sprinkle Holy Absinthe over your trouser press.

Next, you must perform the sacrifice of the trainer. Hold one sports shoe over the Corby and slice open the sole with a cut-throat razor. Shards of synthetic stuffing will drip out, which you must ignite with a Ronson lighter. While the noxious plumes rise, recite the names of famous sportswear brands backwards: "Ekin, Kobeer, Repmac, Lognak!"

Lastly, place the objects in Figure 2 around the voodoo doll representing Mr Headphones. Soon you will witness great changes in him. He will turn up for work in an elegant three-piece worsted suit with a charming silk tie, his brown brogues will gleam with a thousand caresses of the shoe brush, and, despite being a little hard of hearing, he will be the most pleasant, cordial fellow you would care to encounter.

Nails: *Insert a two-inch nail into each ear to induce a surdity, to counteract the absurdity of listening to a walkman.*

Hermes silk: *A scrap of silk placed near the throat will produce a craving for cravats.*

Boot polish: *A few dabs of black polish on the soles of the feet should produce an aversion to modish plimsolls.*

Fig. 2.

FOGGIT'S
PARADE GLOSS
PREMIUM SHOE POLISH
BLACK

Tailor's chalk: *Placed in the groin region, tailor's chalk will induce a powerful urge to have one's inside leg measurements taken.*

GOODY TWO-SHOES

To eradicate this person's tiresome slavery to their desk, two goddesses must be simultaneously evoked and pitted against one another. They are Ceylonia, goddess of tea, and Urethra, goddess of micturation. The ceremony is most effective when performed within the lavatory of a reputable tearoom such as Claridges or the Savoy. You first draw a magick circle on the floor, in which you will remain for the duration of the ritual. Sprinkle some Earl Grey tea (which must be from Fortnum & Mason) into a small saucer of goat's urine and recite the following chant taken from the Tea Party sequence in Alice's Adventures in Wonderland.

"Twinkle twinkle, little bat!
How I wonder what you're at!
Up above the world you fly!
Like a tea tray in the sky."

On the final line, micturate into the toilet bowl while gripping a peacock feather firmly between your teeth. A terrible steam will arise as Ceylonia and Urethra battle it out in the lavatory bowl, but do not be alarmed – it will soon die away and you'll simply be left with a bit of a mess to clear up. When this spell has been performed, Goody Two-Shoes will rarely be seen at his desk. He will divide his time equally between the office lavatorial facilities and the local tearooms, so you'll always know where to find him. ◉

Thesaurus

The poet, inspired by the warm weather to compose epic
odes and lyric poems in his verdant garden

1st May… Mayday celebrations traditionally centred around the garlanded maypole, symbolising the fertile transition into summer.

May Rituals

A gentleman rarely likes to make a fuss. Sending back substandard food in a restaurant or complaining about a neighbour's infernal hip-hop music are chores that a Chap rightly regards with dread, but faced with the relentless march of global capitalism, consumerist vulgarity and the attendant homogenisation of our high streets, a Chap is likely to find his dander swelling to unfeasably large proportions. The advent of a local tearoom being ruthlessly converted into a North American coffee outlet, for example, should be quite enough to push any right-minded citizen tumbling headlong over the edge and make him uncharacteristically willing to indulge in a little protest. The prospect of a man of decorum throwing his lot in with unwashed hippies and adolescent anarchists and taking on the constabulary in Trafalgar Square is too demeaning to contemplate, but converting the traditional rituals of May into an opportunity for the promotion of correct modes of civilised behaviour can be both an attractive and effective way for young men and women to express their ire.

1. Anti-Mobile Men – In a charming routine loosely based on traditional Morris dancing, this plucky troupe of Chaps interprets the outrage experienced by passers-by when encountering that ignoble instrument of shame, the mobile phone. The universal hate-figure of Mobo Dick is symbolically attacked using ceremonial claw-hammers.

2. Dancing round the Barber's Pole – These enthusiastic young ladies are keenly aware that the American penchant for casual clothing, designer stubble and long hair is undermining the very foundations of civilisation. They cavort shamelessly around a phallic barber's pole to express their unerring admiration for traditional male grooming techniques.

3. Beating the Bounders – The medieval practice of 'beating the bounds' took the form of a procession that defined the boundaries of a parish or village. 'Beating the bounders' is a variation on this ritual in which a sturdy band of Chaps enter a branch of Starbucks coffee emporium and drum out pagan rhythms at each corner of the premises, in the hope of reminding customers of the outer limits of what can be regarded as acceptable behaviour.

4. The Hatting of the May Chap – The grand finale of any May celebration is the ceremonial hatting of the fellow who distiguishes himself with the cut and cloth of his bespoke clothing. In a calculated snub to the ghastly purveyors of baseball caps and leisure wear, the winner's head is adorned by the May topper, a highly-decorated creation of considerable beauty.

29th May… Oak Apple Day in Castleton, Derbyshire, when a man dressed as Charles II rides through the town garlanded from head to waist with 56lb of flowers.

Haughty Culture

𝔊𝔞𝔯𝔡𝔢𝔫𝔦𝔫𝔤 𝔴𝔦𝔱𝔥𝔬𝔲𝔱 𝔯𝔢𝔰𝔬𝔯𝔱𝔦𝔫𝔤 𝔱𝔬 𝔤𝔯𝔬𝔴𝔦𝔫𝔤 𝔱𝔥𝔦𝔫𝔤𝔰

𝔗here is no dignity in labour, and any man who claims the contrary is either an utter nincompoop or else an irredeemable scoundrel. This given, it would seem rather unlikely that a man of sound principle would hold any truck with the increasingly popular realm of gardening. It is a pastime that has long been associated with backbreaking toil, unpleasant bending, dirtied clothing and bovine ordure, but despite this we still see hundreds of thousands of gullible amateurs (indoctrinated by television programmes and books dedicated to the subject) stampeding towards so-called 'garden centres' every weekend.

Fig. 1.

Apologists for horticulture might point out that the achievements of such luminaries as John Tradescant and Lancelot 'Capability' Brown should not be glossed over quite so lightly, but it is not the final product of gardening that is at issue here (after all who has not enjoyed wandering through the formal gardens at Cranborne Manor or the idealised landscapes of Blenheim Palace), but more the process by which these results are actually achieved. Messrs Tradescant and Brown were sensible enough to employ bands of mewling minions to run around at their beck and call (shifting vast quantities of humus and dirtying their finger nails in the service of a higher cause), but surely they were as personally unfamiliar with the touch of coarse loam as the average Frenchman is with soap and water.

Taking a leaf from their book, the modern gent should bypass his aversion to the brute vulgarity of practical gardening, not by eschewing horticulture altogether, but by merely adapting it into something less labour intensive and unattractively gritty. In the

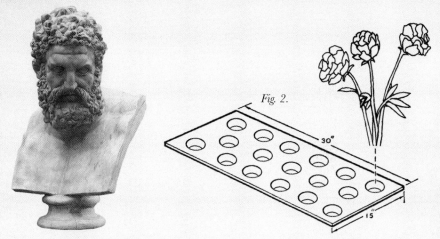

Fig. 2.

absence of legions of staff and anything by the way of a bank balance, a fellow must fall back on his own resourcefulness.

Living as most of us do in the confines of the urban environment, you will, in all likelihood, only have access to a weed stricken patch of wasteland, a neglected roof garden or dingy courtyard, but such confined areas are ideally suited to developing horticultural creativity hemmed in by innate sloth. Converting a guano-spattered light-well into a convincing approximation of an Arcadian glade is a challenging project, but one that can provide immense satisfaction if approached fearlessly and with innovation.

The first rule of gardening with dignity is that a gentleman should have as little as possible to do with growing plants. Showing any kind of compassion towards a plant will only encourage it and make you its slave for life. Days and nights spent in abject nurture will only be responded to by a refusal to prosper or bloom. Rid your mind of such conventional nonsense as planting seeds, pruning, mulching or planning the perfect foliage backdrop for your *Epimedium grandiflorium*, and instead resort to more radical methods. Why grow your own plants when they can be easily obtained ready-made? Get your handyman (*see* Do it, Youssef! page 118) to knock you up an MDF flowerbed, consisting of a sturdy box with holes drilled in the top (Fig. 2) and in each hole place a small spray of cut flowers. Don't be put off by the exorbitant prices that you will see at your local florists. There are far more reliable and cost effective sources of spring and summer blooms. Paying a brief visit to a local park, for example, or availing yourself of abandoned bouquets at your local cemetery should easily satisfy your gardening requirements. The cumulative affect of such a display will come close to rivalling the herbaceous borders of Sissinghurst

Other than involving yourself with ungrateful vegetable matter, colour, vigour and fascination can be imparted into a small outdoor space by several other methods.

In the 18th century, the inclusion of a hermit on one's estate was regarded as the epitome of country house style. There is absolutely no reason why today's dandy should not avail

himself of the same privilege. It's a straightforward enough matter to entice a hopelessly drunken vagrant back to your premises using the simple lure of an opened bottle of wine. Once there, dress him in a bed sheet, wreathe his head in foliage and invite him to take up residence in an old barrel with the promise of unlimited alcohol, tobacco and scraps from your table in return for a sterling display of relentless solitude (Fig. 1). Such a move not only provides the disadvantaged with ideal employment opportunities, but also enhances your reputation for stylish romanticism. Watch your friends gape in wonderment at the picturesque spectacle as your hermit sporadically peers out of the top of the barrel and mutters a few enigmatic words of wisdom.

A similar effect may be achieved by providing members of your local amateur dramatic society with space and an audience to hone their thespian skills. Aspiring 'wannabes' are renowned for their willingness to perform all sorts of menial acting jobs in pursuit of fame and fortune. No money need change hands, the lust for applause and attention is all the incentive they require. With this in mind, invite an attractive young lady to dress up in a rough approximation of Turkish goatherd chic and direct her to stroll across the vast Anatolian plains (some method acting may be required here) with her herd of goats. Due to the domestic proportions of the performance it might be a good idea to 'suggest' the 'herd of goats' by replacing them with a few carefully selected rabbits from a nearby petshop (Fig. 3).

Other than peopling your garden with lyrical recluses, nymphs, dryads and shepherdesses, you should give some thought to the inclusion of garden ornaments. A bust of Apollo or a stone baptismal font will strike the correct note, but prices of such artefacts are now sky high – thanks to the unscrupulousness of architectural salvage merchants. Half-inching these commodities from a church or neighbouring garden is only recommended if you have burly assistance from a chain gang equipped with heavy lifting machinery. Otherwise, you can improvise along a dadaist theme by making challenging constructions out of old rusty bicycles, ironing boards and household plumbing requisites. After all, what is good enough for Mr Duchamp must surely be adequate to satisfy the demands of the art-loving residents of East Sheen.

Fig. 3.

With plumbing items in mind, it is highly recommended that you set up an impressive water feature. There is very little that can rival the merry chuckle of water as it cascades over a gaily painted ballcock, and all that is required is a length of hose pipe and a conveniently placed garden tap. On a hot summer's afternoon, lay back on a hammock, strum your lyre and softly serenade your guests. One and all will be transported on a heavenly cloud to Elysium. ✖

The Churchwarden

This fellow might rightly pride himself on an intimate knowledge of the works Baudelaire, Verlaine and Mallarmé, but by mistreating his staff and affecting an overly long Churchwarden he betrays himself out as a despicable poseur hellbent on petty social snobbery. In an age of egalitarianism, one should never forget to treat the mewling proletariat and assorted hoi polloi as if they were one's social equals.

15th May, 1782… *William Beckford completed work on his Gothick fantasy,* Vathek, *before embarking on a trip to the Continent.*

William Beckford

One of the tragic consequences of an aristocracy on the verge of extinction, is the appalling reduction in the number of follies being built. In the 18th century, follies were springing up all over Britain as readily as branches of McDonald's are today. The greatest of them all was Fonthill Abbey in Wiltshire, built by William Beckford from 1796 to 1822.

This singular fellow had already distinguished himself as an authority on Japanese porcelain and lacquered cabinets. He had also written a splendid Gothic fantasy, *Vathek*, and caused outrage among the aristocracy through his association with William Courtenay, or 'Kitty,' the 3rd Viscount and 9th Earl of Devon. The scandal dashed Beckford's hopes of a peerage and led to a lifetime of self-imposed exile. First to Europe, where he toured the great ancient cities accumulating a vast collection of *objets d'art*, books and curiosities. Upon his return to England, he began construction on a suitable citadel whose proportions would allow him to store his collection and to retreat from the society that had shunned him. "Some people drink to forget their unhappiness," he said. "I do not drink, I build."

The original plan was to construct Fonthill Abbey as an artificial ruined convent with a suite of rooms that could be occupied for entertainments but not permanently. Once work began, however, Beckford and his architect James Wyatt became so engrossed in their project that they decided to construct a folly which would eclipse nearby Salisbury Cathedral in height and splendour. Wyatt based the design of the Abbey on the cruciform of a medieval cathedral, with a central tower 276 feet high (17 feet higher than the top of St Peter's in Rome). All the ground floor rooms led off the great central octagon beneath the tower. Spectacular views stretched through the north-south transept, known as St Michael's Gallery, with a fan-vaulted ceiling based on Henry VII's chapel in Westminster Abbey. Its 300 feet of walls were lined with ebony cabinets containing Beckford's wonderful collection of literature and windows of exquisite stained glass; the only interior lighting came from a profusion of candles in silver candelabra. Beckford extended this extraordinary vista by having the grounds landscaped into avenues of trees.

Visitors to the Abbey were greeted at the vast entrance by Beckford's Swiss dwarf Perro, dressed in a golden coat, to emphasise the height of the doors. Beckford's description in *Vathek* of the Caliph's Abyssinian seraglio, written several years before Fonthill was conceived, could easily have been the Romantic expression of his architectural ambitions: "The palace named The Delight of the Eyes was one entire enchantment. Rarities, collected from every corner of the earth were found in such profusion as to dazzle and confound…"

Once under construction, Fonthill Abbey began to arouse the curiosity of the members of the aristocracy who had ostracised Beckford. His rare visitors to the partially completed building could dine out for months on tales of the eccentric goings-on behind the million trees Beckford had planted in the grounds. Beckford was one of the earliest and most dedicated Romantics, using the grottos, seraglios and secret passages of Arabic folklore as

a backdrop to his tragic and dashing stance. His taste for the Gothic, reflected in his novel *Vathek*, combined with unlimited resources and the inspiration gleaned from his Grand Tour, led to innovations in architecture and interior design that were to influence English interiors until well into the 19th century. The *haute monde* of English society, so quick to ostracise Beckford, were just as eager to adopt his idiosyncratic style for their own palaces, as long as they didn't have to actually meet the fellow.

James Wyatt had approached the construction of Fonthill Abbey as if it really were a Gothic cathedral, to the extent that some of the materials he used were authentically medieval. The result was that although Fonthill may have resembled the dream palace of the 9th Caliph of the Abbasides, structurally it was more similar to a garden shed. Wood and cement were used in place of stone and too little research had been made into building 276-ft cathedral-eclipsing towers. These defects led to the central tower of Fonthill collapsing twice during construction. Three years after Beckford sold it, the tower collapsed a third time, turning the Abbey into what he had originally intended: a ruined convent in the middle of a wood.

All that remains today of Fonthill Abbey is a magnificent pile of rubble in Wiltshire, but while it stood, it was the most magnificent paean to Gothic self-indulgence that ever existed in Britain – the nearest construction this side of Constantinople to attain a glimpse of the splendours of old Araby.

"When the workmen had raised the structure a cubit in the day time, two cubits more were added in the night. The expedition with which the fabric arose was not a little flattering to the vanity of Vathek: *he fancied that even insensible matter shewed a forwardness to subserve his designs, not considering that the success of the foolish and wicked form the first rod of their chastisement."* William Beckford, *Vathek*.

Epicurus

The food lover, who begins foraging around for ingredients
for the season's lavish picnics

Pater Divining

𝕿𝖍𝖊 𝖆𝖗𝖙 𝖔𝖋 𝖉𝖎𝖘𝖈𝖔𝖛𝖊𝖗𝖎𝖓𝖌 𝖜𝖍𝖔'𝖘 𝖙𝖍𝖊 𝕯𝖆𝖉𝖉𝖞 𝖎𝖓 𝖙𝖍𝖊 𝖋𝖆𝖒𝖎𝖑𝖞 𝖍𝖔𝖒𝖊𝖘𝖙𝖊𝖆𝖉

𝔚e too easily make assumptions about the respective identities of our family members. Absently handing an empty teacup to mother, we request assistance with crosswords from uncle Hubert, and when it comes to asking permission to use the family car for a day trip to Bognor, we always turn to father. But how can we really be sure which one really is the Old Man?

Take a look at the occupants of a typical family home – any one of them could be your father, despite appearances to the contrary. That middle-aged fellow in the armchair, for instance, his receding barnet staining the antimacassar with a sepia halo. There may be something distinctly avuncular in the absorbed way he is filling his pipe, but can you be sure that he is not, in actual fact, your father? Consider the lady in a frilly pinafore constantly bustling in and out of the kitchen, whose tired eyes light up as she hands you a plate of hot macaroons, fresh from the oven. There is no earthly reason why this too should not be your dad, for in these enlightened times we are told not to make assumptions about gender based on physical attributes. And look, yonder in the garden. Who's that sprightly cove in a pair of shorts playing tennis with a young lady? Who are you to say that neither of them is your dear papa?

We have devised a clear set of guidelines to assist the confused son or daughter in divining who is the genuine patriarch of the typical family household.

THE GENTLEMEN'S TACTIC

One of the most reliable preliminaries to divine the state of fatherhood is to engage the suspected person in conversation. There are vital clues to look out for in his or her speech. For example, should the person display extremist political views that ten years ago you would have found deplorably bigoted, yet now seem reassuringly appealing and grounded in common sense – there is strong evidence that this could be your father.

Be vigilant in your wanderings around the house for any excessive tinkering activity. Fathers are deeply attached to minor repairs and enjoy nothing more than 'doing it themselves'. Should you hear, on the family grapevine, of a new set of shelves being erected in the spare bedroom, make an investigation *toute de suite*. As you mount the stairs to the sounds of drilling mingled with a whistled wartime ditty echoing from beyond the bedroom door, you can almost be certain that behind it your father is at work.

The happy members of a typical family – but how can you be sure which one is the patriarch?

Should you enter, however, and find someone you could swear was your cousin Tabitha drilling holes into the wall, wearing a gymslip and white plimsolls with her hair in pigtails – do not give up, for this could still be your father, in playful dressing-up mode.

But the general rules concerning clothes are that if the suspected person's dress sense is an eccentric, slightly scruffier version of your own sartorial style, then this could be your man.

If you're still not sure, ask a few more specific questions. Do you find, as you probe more deeply into this person's mind, perhaps touching upon a few emotive matters, that he visibly flinches, glances at his watch and mutters something about listening to Gardeners' Question Time? If, when pressed to give an answer to a question such as, "Why, when I was a child, was mother always going on holiday with Uncle Hubert?" your quarry begins to gasp for air, suddenly remembering that the lawn mower is in urgent need of repair, then, by jingo, it looks like you've found him! A way of dispelling all uncertainty is to resort to the final Shibboleth, the mystical phrase that will always guarantee a father revealing his identity to his son or daughter, "Pater, can I borrow fifty grand?"

It goes without saying that if the answer is no, then you've found your man.

THE LADIES' APPROACH

The ladies will probably have less difficulty extracting funds from the paterfamilias, for pressing wads of fivers into his daughter's hand makes him feel useful, but there are a whole host of other techniques you can try. One is to request that each member of the family spend a few minutes alone in a room with you. If any of them become agitated and uncomfortable, then you might be on to something. Watch out for signs such as fidgeting, avoiding eye contact or suddenly squatting down to examine a crack in the skirting board.

Disapproving comments on your clothing are also an indicator of paternity. If the person under suspicion narrows his eyes and says, "That's a bit summery, isn't it?" when you're wearing a full-length sleeveless dress from Laura Ashley, he might very well be your father. Uncle Hubert would merely give a lascivious wink and complement you on your figure.

Another reliable test is when you arrive at the family home by car. The man who spreads a map on the kitchen table as you walk in the door and insists on a detailed description of your route, tracing it on the map with the stem of his pipe – this is probably your Papa.

The real litmus test of paternity, though, is when you bring a new paramour to meet your parents. The hearty fellow who invites your beau into the study to "crack open the 15-year-old Talisker and a pair of pre-Castro Cohibas I've been saving for a special occasion" is more likely to be your Uncle Hubert. Your dad is the man lurking awkwardly in the corner while the introductions are being made, who disappears into the garden shed as soon as tea is served, only to reappear as you and your beau are leaving.

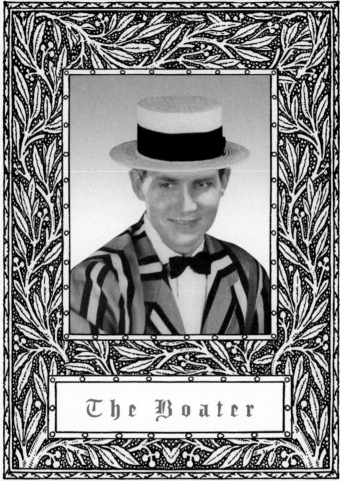

The Boater

That reassuringly egalitarian piece of headwear, the Boater is equally at home balanced upon the bonces of butchers, fishmongers, members of a barber shop quartet or languid poets enjoying a lazy summer jaunt down the river on a punt. Any hat adaptable enough to embody values of Epicurianism, personal grooming and complete inertia should surely be regarded as the papal crown of masculine haberdashery.

The Brothers of Perpetual Indulgence

𝕷𝖊𝖙 𝖚𝖘 𝖊𝖆𝖙 𝖆𝖓𝖉 𝖉𝖗𝖎𝖓𝖐, 𝖋𝖔𝖗 𝖙𝖔𝖒𝖔𝖗𝖗𝖔𝖜 𝖜𝖊 𝖘𝖍𝖆𝖑𝖑 𝖉𝖎𝖊
(**𝕻𝖘𝖆𝖑𝖒𝖘** XXII)

On the outskirts of a small village near Bruges, Belgium, may be found the Abbey of La Chappe, the home of a monastic brotherhood devoted to drunkenness and the high life. The Order of La Chappe was founded in 1964 by the Benedictine scholar, master brewer and dipsomaniac Father Pilsner of Bruges. Father Pilsner's aim was to reject the austerities imposed on the lives of monks by the Rule of St Benedict, unaltered since the 6th century. Father Pilsner created a new Rule more in keeping with the needs of today's monk as well as allowing the Chappist monk to devote himself to a life of bodily indulgence without becoming too fragile.

The first aspect of the Rule of St Benedict to get a major overhaul by Father Pilsner was the unsociable hours. A Benedictine monk was expected to rise at 2.30 in the morning for Matins, followed by Lauds, Prime, Terce, Sext, Vespers and Compline, with bedtime at 7pm. The new monastic timetable recommended by Father Pilsner was as follows.

Martinis, 12pm – The day begins with a stiff dry martini to dust away the cobwebs of sleep and prepare the monk for a day of heavy drinking and larking about.

Lords, 1pm – The monks quite simply get drunk as lords, while slurring the 118th Psalm in preparation for luncheon.

Prime Repast, 2–4pm – The main meal of the day, incorporating eight or nine courses accompanied by tankards of the fortified ales brewed at the Abbey.

Naps, 4–5pm – The monks repair to the dormitory to sleep off their luncheon, accompanied by a large tumbler of Armagnac.

Gaspers, 5pm – The monks repair to the Smoking Room for an hour of communion with Lady Nicotine.

Libations, 6–8pm – Pick-me-ups are taken in the Chapel of Higher Worship, a fully equipped tavern-style bar with a choice of 17 different ales.

Carousal, 9pm–3am – The longest part of the monastic day, when the monks show their adoration for the Divine One by getting up to all sorts of high jinks and tomfoolery.

The monks are supposed to retire at 3am. This can be a long and drawn out process, as most of them are so inebriated that they have difficulty finding their way back to the dormitory. Many fall asleep in the corridors or the former herb garden, while others go wandering off to bother the nuns in the convent next door. It should be noted that, while the Abbey encourages drunkenness of the greatest intensity, they have no truck with loutishness. Thus, certain temptations are put in the paths of the drunken novitiates to test their devotion. A supply of traffic cones and lavatory seats are placed tantalisingly near dummy lampposts in the herb garden. If a monk is unable to curb his desire to climb the lamppost with a traffic cone on his head, he must attend confession the next day and request absolution from the Abbot.

Another part of the Rule of St Benedict amended by Father Pilsner was the monks' attire. He commissioned Huntsman of Savile Row to design some rather elegant bespoke habits. He chose an extremely coarse Harris Tweed for the habit and cowl, as a sort of homage to the itchy hessian habits endured by the Benedictines. The scapular features a smooth, silken surface that is both stylish and easily wiped clean in the event of spillages. Trickers of Jermyn Street designed some wonderful brogues in precisely the same shade of nut-brown as Father Pilsner's favourite monastic ale, a Bosteels' Karmeliet *tripel*.

NUNC EST BIBENDUM

But what is the point of all this? Why found an abbey exclusively devoted to drinking and carousing, for surely there is enough of that in the secular world already? Father Pilsner, now in his eighties but still the active Abbot of La Chappe, explains, while sipping from an enormous tankard of copper-coloured ale:

"When St Benedict created his Rule in the 6th century, it was in response to a need for the daily life of a monk to be brought up to date. Monks were still living according to the dictates of Egyptian ascetics from three centuries earlier, when a meal of three olives, two prunes and a fig was considered a sumptuous repast. Now that we are in the 21st century, I believe that the Rule of St Benedict is hopelessly out of date, and I have created my own new Rule.

"The Rule of Father Pilsner states, in 73 chapters, that the glorious bounty of God's good earth is being too neglected in secular life. Ordinary people are shunning the joys of

tobacco, rich foods and strong ales in favour of a healthy lifestyle, in the belief that their austerity will ensure a longer mortal life. This may be true, but I wonder what their chances are of a place in the afterlife, when their souls have been impoverished in fitness clubs and juice bars? We at the Order of La Chappe believe that it is only through overindulgence in the pleasures of temporal life that we can achieve unity with the Divine One and an assurance of a place in the Celestial Realm of Permanent Intoxication.

"As for our much-discussed choice of tipple, I can only refer you to the tradition of monastic breweries in Benedictine times, when monks drank strong beers to sustain them through the fastings of Lent. Today, at the Abbey of La Chappe, our brethren are drinking even stronger ales to endure the perpetual period of spiritual fasting that has come to define the activities of the secular world."

O NOCTES CENAE DEUM

So what does it take to become a novitiate at the Abbey of La Chappe? In the first instance, the candidate must be a single male, baptized a Christian and already zealously living the life of an epicure and heavy drinker. He must have scandalised his parents at least three times and he must receive the consent of his local publican before he is ready to enter the monastery. He must have a very high tolerance for alcohol, strong cheeses, heavy sauces, viands, sickly desserts and sweetmeats. He must not be given to excessive chattering and waffle, being more concerned with the higher tasks of eating and drinking.

Once ordained, each monk is assigned specific duties at the Abbey. The younger novitiates staff the breweries, manned 24 hours a day to keep up with monastic demand. Novitiates learn all aspects of ale production as well as the subtle art of beer tasting; how to describe, for example, the complex caramel flavour with hints of raisins and a chocolatey aroma of an *oud bruin*.

When he has mastered the skills of brewing, the novitiate may progress to a role involving more contact with other monks, such as barman in the tavern or maitre d' in the refectory. Some of the monks prefer more academic roles and will be permitted to apply for a position in the Scriptorium. After the refectory, the Scriptorium is the most important building in the Abbey. It is where the sacred texts of Chappist literature are stored for the monks to affirm their devotion to the High Life. These periods of sacred study are known as *Lectio Divina*, and are always accompanied a glass of Benedictine. The period begins with a reading of the Chappist liturgy from A E Housman.

And Malt does more than Milton can
To justify God's ways to man.
Ale, man, ale's the stuff to drink
For fellows whom it hurts to think

The monk will then move on to a reading of a more lengthy work, such as an epic poem by one of the Romantic poets or a novel by one of the great dipsomaniac authors like F Scott Fitzgerald or Malcolm Lowry.

Ut Sint Vina Proxima

There are further physical pleasures to be enjoyed at the monastery. Next door to the Abbey is the Chappistine Convent of Notre Dame des Vins Fins, whose aims are similar to the Chappists. The nuns cultivate excellent vineyards and ferment crisp white wines, such as Chardonnay and Sauvignon Blanc. The structure of devotion at the convent is not unlike that of the Abbey, with the exception that their Chapel of Higher Worship is a wine bar rather than a tavern. Also, the convent's former chapter house has been converted into a small shopping mall with branches of Zara and French Connection.

There is a gap in the wall that separates the Abbey from the convent (it is widely supposed that Father Pilsner himself removed the bricks one drunken night). The resulting orifice permits easy access in both directions, and as soon as Carousal is finished and the lights of both dormitories have been extinguished, so the pleasures of the flesh are enjoyed in fumbled assignations in the former herb gardens. While not actively encouraged by the Abbot, these trysts are tolerated, since any form of physical pleasure can only bring the monks closer to Heaven.

The Abbey of La Chappe is a strictly cloistered order with no active apostolate; the monks do not mingle with the populace or proselytise. Once ordained, they are expected to remain at the Abbey until their mortal end. With the punishing rituals of drinking, smoking and unhealthy eating, life expectancy peaks at around 39 or 40. Many young people these days, observing their peers self-righteous attitudes towards intoxication and high living, are increasingly drawn towards the credo of the Chappist Order. The promise it offers of eternal communion with the angels in Heaven, as well as a damn good, if a little brief, jamboree here on Earth, seems to be a temptation they are finding difficult to resist. Ⓧ

Portion Control

Fig. 1.

℣ℌℯ clement weather of June may present itself as an ideal opportunity to throw off the trammels of urban living and set off in one's motor car in an attempt 'to get away from it all'. Embarking upon the open highway in pursuit of sand, sea and sun is a purposeless and hazardous venture at the best of times, but the traveller should beware that the pitfalls of traffic jams, fatal collisions, sun burn and drowning are not the only threats we are likely to encounter upon the way. Extended journeys will inevitably involve a lot of eating out at restaurants and cafés, and if you are exceptionally unlucky, motorway services. Being unfamiliar with an area can sometimes lead a gentleman into grave arenas of culinary danger.

Walking into a roadside eatery, an unsuspecting fellow is likely find himself confronted by a menace that is currently seeping its poison into the bloodstream of the nation. It is a silent plague that is corroding the very foundations of a man's self-esteem. It is called 'portion control'.

As is the case with many injurious concepts, this one hails from the United States of America, and is the hideous euphemism for the individual packaging in sachets, mini-cartons and horrible little plastic containers of a variety of comestible items from sugar, butter and milk to jam, honey and sauces. It remains unclear the exact nature of the dark forces that are at work here and precisely what they hope to achieve by visiting such knavery upon us, but as the name suggests, portion control is an infringement of man's fundamental right to gormandise and is a puritanical plot by shadowy organisations against those three major tenets of a decadent gentleman's belief system: freedom, style and excess.

PSYCHOLOGY

On your travels through life you will no doubt have ventured upon, in railway cafés and down-trodden eateries, little old ladies vainly endeavouring to make their gnarled, old,

arthritic talons do their bidding. Here, in their twilight years, old ladies should be treated with gentleness and respect, but instead they are forced, like performing chimpanzees at a sadist's tea party, to demean themselves by exploding diminutive cartons of milk up their nostrils or squirting sachets of brown sauce all over their astrakhan collars.

Even for the more nimble-fingered amongst us the contest between prehensile digit and sachet can be a daunting one. Try entertaining a young lady with sparkling conversation whilst simultaneously trying to separate a wafer thin container of ketchup from its tomatoey contents. Sir, it cannot be done.

It seems that someone, somewhere is playing with our thought processes and eroding our self-confidence. Portion control turns us all into paupers at the banquet of life, forcing us to subsist on meagre offerings, calculated to make us believe that we are not worthy to dine on the decently proportioned servings we truly deserve.

ERGONOMICS

Whichever sinister ministry or occultist conspiracy came up with the idea of portion control in the first place, it is patently obvious that it was designed solely to inconvenience and humiliate the users of such products, stripping them of the will to live like gentlemen.

We all, once in a while, due to the vagaries of travel, find ourselves in barbaric foreign locales (such as Coventry or Dagenham) where we are forced through the inadequate provision of proper eating houses to enter establishments known as 'self-service restaurants'. Instead of having one's pot of oolong, milk, sugar, butter and toasted teacake brought to one's table by an enchanting young village girl, one is required to scrabble about at a stainless-steel counter vying with other customers to gain the attention of diffident staff. Serious mental agility is required at this juncture to determine the exact combination of sachets, plastic containers and foil-wrapped nutrients that will be required to satisfy one's gastronomic needs. Many pressing questions will have to be answered: Exactly how many sachets of sugar make a teaspoonful? How many foil-clad dollops of butter are enough to charge the blade of an average knife? How many mini milk cartons approximates a decently-sized sploosh from a delicately patterned porcelain jug? Who on earth uses non-fat milk, ersatz sugar and 'I can't believe it's not inedible' butter in the first place?

Having done one's mathematics, one is then required to pad about like a vagrant trying to carry one's individually wrapped booty and find a free table. Even when this is accomplished, frequent visits back to the counter are required in order to finally end up with something that vaguely approximates a fully rounded meal. This is, of course, where the restaurateur relies very much on the all-important 'guilt factor' – hoping that his customers will be far too self-conscious and bashful to request many more condiment items.

GASTRONOMICS

The proof of the pudding is in the eating, and if this particular pudding was presented as evidence in a high court of gastronomy, then its purveyors would be found very guilty indeed of perjury, fraud and grievous bodily harm against a Chap's taste buds.

"Show me the individually wrapped portion of processed cheese before 11, and I'll show you the dyspepsia," goes the old Jesuit adage. And surely these muscular Christians were on to something.

Strangely enough, confining food for a month or so in a tight plastic envelope gives food all the flavour of... a tight plastic envelope.

STANDING UP AND BEING COUNTED

Nobody wishes to be taken for a fool, and such cynical treatment at the hands of the restaurant trade is apt to make a man's blood run cold. Clandestine forces are obviously afoot, and if we are not to be turned into weak-willed slaves we should resolve to fight fire with fire.

It is a relatively simple matter, in establishments where sachets and mini-cartons are displayed freely in a plastic trough, to grab as many items as possible, filling one's pockets and one's fists, and transporting them back to your table. Here, under the cover of an opened menu, swiftly transfer the contents of the milk cartons into an attractive pottery jug, which you will have secreted upon your person prior to entering. Likewise, a carefully concealed butter-dish may be whipped out in a trice and the contents of those nasty foil wraps installed therein. If you're feeling particularly creative, as an added touch of bravura, why not engrave this newly crafted block of butter with a pleasant rustic design involving cows and ears of wheat.

In cafés where extra sachets must be asked for, be bold and return repeatedly to the bar or counter every three minutes for a period of 40 minutes or so requesting extra portions of this or that, demanding replacements or politely venturing that the contents of a particular sachet might be 'a little bit off'. In short, counteract the 'guilt factor' with the 'bloody nuisance factor'. Be wary, landlords and catering staff have been known to become restive and physically threatening under such provocation. Persevere, but tread carefully.

If you find yourself temperamentally unsuited to direct confrontation, it is perfectly possible to enter the fray with more circumspection. One suggestion would be to pursue a course of subversive labelling. Make a number of photocopies of the corrosive chemical warning sign from a household bottle of bleach and, armed with a suitably quick-drying glue, adhere the label to as many items of portion control as is conveniently practical, before placing them back in their storage container (Fig. 1). Undermining consumers' faith in these products of infamy is not only richly satisfying to a man of taste and dignity, but is also a public service to benighted hoi polloi sadly unaware that their immortal souls are gradually being siphoned away into a pit of banality. ⊗

Pan

Lover of nature, he is to be found lurking in forest glades
with leaves in his hair and dirt on his hands

Feral Chaps

No serious student of natural history could be unaware of reports concerning the existence of feral varieties of chap who are rumoured to inhabit the more remote regions of the globe. Numerous eye-witness accounts and a growing dossier of photographic evidence bear witness to the authenticity of such encounters, yet there is still a great deal of scepticism in the mainstream of so-called 'science' that dismisses the existence of these creatures out of hand. If a hardcore of stubborn egg-heads insist on the presentation of proof and verification, then surely proof and verification must be given. As usual, we find ourselves up to the challenge.

For centuries, anecdotal evidence of wild men has featured in the mythology of many continents. Who can honestly say that they are not aware of the Abominably Drollman (otherwise known as The Witti) who has often been spotted roaming about the snowy peaks of the Himalayas tossing his urbane epigrams into the sub-zero winds? Whose imagination has remained untouched by reports of the Mild Man of Borneo, that majestic gent of the jungle swinging nonchalantly from bough to bough? Who hasn't been moved by accounts of Sloshscotch (or Brogue Foot) that inebriated, but immaculately dressed, giant of North America who lumbers around in a state of permanent malt-whisky-fuelled intoxication?

Imagine how thrilled we were to learn of a group of feral chaps who dwell far closer to home. It has come to our notice that a tribe of disenchanted Lloyds 'names', cut loose from society by the financial difficulties of the late 1980s, have now 'gone native' in Holland Park, a modest piece of

Fig. 1. This young feral chap doesn't allow the rigors of tree dwelling to dampen his innate ardour for dandyism.

wasteland in west London. Realising the errors of their dismal and unimaginative pursuit of mammon and thoroughly chastened by bankruptcy, these formerly unattractive individuals now dwell in a state of faux-rural grandeur, doing 'what comes naturally'.

As a special treat for the summer months, we recommend that the enthusiastic amateur could do worse than stride out to Holland Park, telephoto appendage in hand, helping us to gather incontrovertible proof which could turn zoological orthodoxy on its head.

With this in mind, we commissioned Professor Compton Pauncefoot of the Institute of Obfuscational Studies to look into the matter and were delighted by the extraordinary photographic record that he returned with.

Fig. 2. A dominant male holds his chapette in a protective embrace. Keeping a sharp lookout for rival suitors will occupy most of a feral chap's day during the summer months.

It was immediately apparent to Professor Pauncefoot that from a very limited genetic pool of five or six mating pairs, an impressive colony of feral chaps has taken root. These shy and largely nocturnal 'gentlemen of the glade' can prove pretty difficult to spot during the winter months when they remain hidden away from view in a state of hibernation. It is in high summer that they usually make their presence felt. This is for several reasons, but chief among them is the quest for a mate. During a mating season that lasts from early spring to late autumn the industrious feral male will demonstrate his eligibility as a suitor by erecting a structure known as a 'nest' or 'des res'. The female of the species will only consider a male who demonstrates architectural finesse and well-developed aesthetic sensibilities in the construction of this nest. This is usually along rigid neo-Palladian lines and is built 10–14 feet above the ground in a suitably shaped tree. (Fig. 3). There is also a great deal of prestige attached to an abode that is located in the fashionable north end of the park away from the hubbub of Kensington High Street. Dominant males who build in this area have to protect their des reses fiercely. Stiff competition is guaranteed.

Generally speaking, conflict between rival males takes the form of 'badinage'. Contestants for a lady's affections draw themselves up to full height and signal their presence to each other by smoking a particularly pungent variety of navy shag. Contact having been made, the contest begins. A careless quip may start off the encounter, followed by a rapidly escalating exchange consisting of louche axioms, frisky witticisms, jaunty banter and withering sarcasm. To blush, hesitate or stumble will mean instant humiliation and defeat, as will an inability to make the female gasp in wonderment at sentiments pithily expressed.

Fig. 3. A feral chap 'nest'. Constructed from salvage materials and of a pleasing neo-Palladian design.

The offspring are born throughout the year and Professor Pauncefoot's observations seem to suggest that a younger generation of feral chap are adapting well to their outdoor existence. Much to the chagrin of their parents, they have abandoned the wearing of suits (which have been replaced by impressive hair growth), but this does not prevent them from still following the essential tenets of taste and dandyism (Fig. 1). The energy and enthusiasm of this new generation are essential for the continuing survival of the group. By night, they are sent by their parents to forage for food in the capacious wheely-bins behind the food hall at Harrods. Here, a providential crop of out-of-date commestible items, such as fois gras, delicate patisserie, smoked salmon and English farmhouse cheeses, form the essential requirements of their dietary needs. Even though a feral chap's standards may be very different from our own, it would surely be beneath the dignity of any human being to have to survive solely on a diet of leaves and vegetable matter. Now *that* would be beyond the pale. 🐝

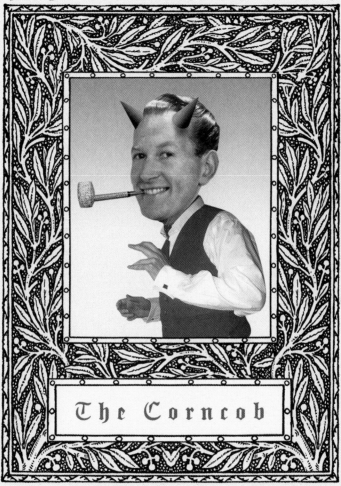

The Corncob

 Nothing can quite compare to the stimulating effects of a rough shag in the open countryside. This fellow lets his spirits soar by sallying forth with an appropriately rustic smoking implement clenched firmly between his teeth, cocking a snook at bourgeois convention. Counteracting the injurious effects of fresh air and filling one's head with tobaccotine melodies, corncobs should surely be regarded as the real 'pipes of Pan'.

Picnic Feng Shui

The allure of the great outdoors has always been something that a Chap finds reasonably easy to resist, but with the onset of high summer the chances are your lady love will suggest a spot of *déjeuner sur l'herbe à deux*. Stumbling into the countryside ill-prepared is fraught with danger. The prevalence of wasps and fresh air, and a complete dearth of proper seating can lead to much pain and discomfort. Insect repellent, a shooting stick and a large packet of fags can go some way to alleviating these irritations, but for a more holistic remedy to the unpleasantness of the outdoors we recommend recourse to the ancient wisdom of the East. Picnic Feng Shui allows you to harness the invisible energy of the cosmos, the Chi, in order to ordain your rural shenanigans with a damn sight more harmony and tranquillity than the bleak aspect of the countryside might lead you to expect. A gingham cloth carefully interacting with the flow and order of the universe, the Tao, will ensure a great sense of wellbeing.

The simple scheme opposite represents the ideal positioning of the essential elements of a good picnic. You will note that the chap (A) places himself diagonally opposite to his beloved (B) on a northeast-northwesterly axis. An unenlightened lady may query your decision to bring along Ahmed, your Moroccan boy servant, but as any skilled geomancer will tell you, as long as he resides within the confines of the pipe radius, he can add nothing but positive energy to the proceedings. What's more, he will prove invaluable for scampering about retrieving comestible items and drinks.

As the afternoon progresses, you may feel impelled by some inexplicable urge to give vent to self-expression via the medium of dance. This should take the form of a light foxtrot performed along a diagonal tract adjacent to the gramophone, the Terpsichorean meridian, specifically reserved for such purposes. The injurious consequences of physical exertion can be effectively neutralised at this point by keeping one's Yin and Yang under a tight rein through the auspices of several large post-prandial single malts.

N

害 本

Winter ~ Fire

Picnic hamper

B

comestible axis

Autumn ~ Gin

Gramophone

Terpsichorean meridian

Spring ~ Earth

Moroccan boy servant

Drinks cabinet

A

pipe radius

Summer ~ Tonic

Baron Corvo

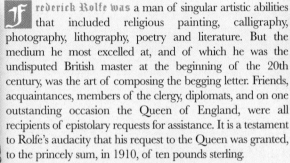

Frederick Rolfe was a man of singular artistic abilities that included religious painting, calligraphy, photography, lithography, poetry and literature. But the medium he most excelled at, and of which he was the undisputed British master at the beginning of the 20th century, was the art of composing the begging letter. Friends, acquaintances, members of the clergy, diplomats, and on one outstanding occasion the Queen of England, were all recipients of epistolary requests for assistance. It is a testament to Rolfe's audacity that his request to the Queen was granted, to the princely sum, in 1910, of ten pounds sterling.

Rolfe's artistic career was severely marred by an almost pathological inability to make any money. The few earnings from his artistic endeavours he soon frittered away on costly cigarettes, ecclesiastical raiment and luxury goods. He had difficulty in making friends, and when he did so, the relationship invariably followed an identical pattern. Someone would initially be charmed by Rolfe's eccentric appearance and his archaic manner of speaking, and beguiled by his unusual tales peppered with classical references and liturgical knowledge. Rolfe could never resist unloading the details of his financial difficulties into any conversation, so that after a single meeting the listener was convinced they were in the presence of a genius who could flourish if only given the opportunity.

Rolfe's encounters often resulted in a brief period of financial support while he produced a novel or a series of paintings. This would be followed by an argument with his benefactor over some trifle (in one case, the news that his novel was to be typeset by a Quaker – Rolfe was a devout Catholic). The next and final stage of the relationship was a series of letters, postcards and telegrams to the erstwhile companion, showering him with spite and vitriol and accusations of gross misconduct and betrayal.

Rolfe's earliest series of letters were written at Collegio Scozzese in Rome, where he was sent, aged 29, to be ordained into the priesthood. After five months, his burgeoning interest in painting and poetry ostracised him from the other students, and he brought shame upon the college by running up huge bills with local artist's suppliers and tailors. When threatened with expulsion, he wrote to the college rector protesting the decision.

"Now that your sentence of dismissal has been carried out, you have refused to hear the explanations I have to offer. You and my diocesan have refused me what every Christian principle of justice demands, viz. an unbiased hearing and a fair trial, the right of the lowest felon. I ask once more, are you going to see me starve in the streets? Is such a scandal to go on indefinitely?"

Rolfe's plea was answered by expulsion a few weeks later. Refusing to get out of bed, he was deposited, mattress and all, on the street outside the college.

Rolfe's next epistolary opus was begun at the small town of Holywell in Wales, where one Father Beauclerk had commissioned him to paint some banners. The results were remarkable for the fact that every one of the 149 saints depicted on the banners bore the identical large-nosed, myopic face of Rolfe himself. Some confusion arose when Rolfe was told that board and lodging would be the only payment for painting the banners. He responded by sending Fr Beauclerk a bill for £1000 and a barrage of furious letters.

"Dear Fr. Beauclerk,
I know that it is impossible for me to get on. You have taken care of that, since you made me a physical wreck by 21 months of slavery in squalor; a mental wreck by destroying my faith in all men (for if the highest rank, viz. the clergy, will brazenly defraud a man of the promised fruits of his labour I have no faith left for the others) and a spiritual wreck by keeping me from the Sacraments for eight months.
> *F. Austin"*

Even the adoption of a pseudonym had done nothing to prevent Rolfe's name becoming mud, once again, in the Catholic Church. He found himself penniless and rejected by the citizenry of Holywell. Realising that a secular career was his only option, he changed his name again, but this time to one that signalled a real break with his past, and with connotations both heraldic and mythological: Baron Corvo was born.

The next series of letters were to John Lane, publisher of *The Yellow Book*, who had printed a few of Baron Corvo's short stories. *"Having executed certain works of art,"* Corvo wrote, *"at the commission of a Jesuit of note, who promised to pay me generously, and buoyed me up with promises, I was flabbergasted when he turned around and said he couldn't pay but would give me a few pounds in charity."*

The details of Corvo's personal life were of little interest to a busy London publisher, but Lane was intrigued by the author of the stories he had published and invited him for a visit to his offices. Having no means to pay for the five-hour rail journey to London, Corvo set off on foot, dressed in a worn corduroy suit and withered cloak, a home-made skull-cap, black slippers and socks of corvine purple. Lane noted that Corvo's socks and fingernails were always clean and his appearance neat and concise, despite the shabby suit and shoes. The meeting resulted in a second edition of Corvo's Toto stories, bound with Max Beerbohm's *The Happy Hypocrite*.

Corvo's next commission was a chronicle of the rise and fall of the Italian Borgia family. His relations with its editor, Grant Richards, followed precisely the same pattern as ever.

Initial cordiality and cooperation soon turned to bitterness and audacity when Corvo decided that a completely revised version of his own book was necessary – for which he would charge £273 (on top of an initial fee of £48 for the commissioned work). Richards' refusal resulted, naturally, in a heated series of letters from the unhappy author, especially when the unrevised edition of his book appeared in print. At the time, Corvo was lodging with a Catholic solicitor named Edward Slaughter, who had kindly invited the impecunious writer to take a spare room at his Hampstead home.

This act of kindness was somehow transformed, in Corvo's deluded mind, into a species of professional agreement. Slaughter made a few enquiries to Richards as to the possibility of selling the Borgia chronicle to another publisher, thus opening yet another seam of Corvo's wrath. *"Will you kindly note,"* he wrote to Richards, *"that I disapprove of and entirely dissociate myself from Mr Edward Slaughter's ridiculous mismanagement of my affairs. I find that my confidence once more has been abused by a stupid and dishonourable Roman Catholic. In seventeen years I have never met one R.C., except the Bishop of Menevia, who was not a sedulous ape, a treacherous snob, a slanderer, an oppressor, or a liar; and I am going to try to do without them."*

Baron Corvo's final, and most notorious, series of letters came from his adopted home of Venice. In this romantic city he was to find fulfilment of the desires he had suppressed through lifelong celibacy – the last vestige of his almost extinguished desire for ordination. He befriended Venice's gondoliers, photographing these athletic, tanned young fellows in quasi-religious or mythological poses. The legendary Venice letters chronicle his activities with the gondoliers after sundown, when the former tonsured cleric devoted himself to the vices available in the dark byways of the ancient city.

But he still found time to wreak vengeance on imagined enemies. His many benefactors in Venice later appeared as libellous caricatures in his final novel, *The Desire and Pursuit of the Whole*, and the bilious letters to former benefactors never ceased.

The most extraordinary of these was written from Corvo's temporary home, a tiny garret in an alleyway infested with rats. *"I possess a Foreign Office Passport,"* he wrote to the British Consul in Venice, *"requiring all whom it may concern to afford me every assistance and protection of which I may stand in need. I have therefore to ask reluctantly for your official intervention. All that is necessary is to appoint and instruct a competent person in England to take over my obligations and assets and to let me have a chance to resume my work."*

The reply stated that Mr Rolfe had understood the terms of his passport too literally, and that no action could be taken in the matter.

Corvo died while removing his shoes on 25th October 1913. Three years of living alternately in damp attics, dusty landings and under an upturned boat on the Lido had brought on a pulmonary pneumonia.

"My opinion, Eminency, is that I have a divine vocation for the priesthood... I am not one of your low Erse or pseudo Gaels, flibbertigibbets of frothy or flighty fervour, whom you can blow hither and thither with a sixpence for a fan. Thank the Lord I'm English, born under Cancer, tenacious, slow and sure. Naturally I persist. Fr. Rolfe, Hadrian VII."

Languida

The idle fellow who spends the sultry months laying about
on faded chaise longues in crumbling European cities

International Hand Signals

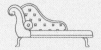

'**A**broad is bloody' according to that dissolute old librarian, Phillip Larkin. Ideed it is, but that does not prevent millions of us relinquishing hold of Terra Britannica each summer and stepping out onto foriegn soil. For the Englishman abroad, sign language, a trusty riding crop and speaking very loudly indeed usually ensure that he is never deprived of the bare essentials of civilised existence: a roof over his head, the constituent ingredients of an expertly constructed dry martini and a large pot of Thedgeley's Chunky-Cut "Olde Time" Marmalade. But merely 'getting by' has never been an adequate way for a genleman to conduct his affairs. It is surely high time that the various gestures a fellow falls back on were formalised into a structured, internationally recognised sign language that is both clear of meaning and elegant of usage.

International Hand Signals act as a mute and stylish mime-Esperanto, destined to become a universal *lingua franca* that will spread understanding, cordiality and harmony between individuals and nations. On travels in treacherous locales where the English language is seldom spoken, such as Chechnya, Colombia or Middlesborough, a thorough grounding in IHS will surely prevent all sorts of misunderstandings and unpleasantness.

THE HITCHER

Standing at the side of the road making an ass of oneself is best left to students and other assorted riffraff. A man of worth, stranded through lack of petrol, is prepared to hike 10 miles to the nearest garage rather than subject himself to such indignity.

THE AESTHETE

Swooning is a laudable pastime for any young fellow who finds himself at odds with the modern obsessions of consumerism and greed. Signifying 'The Muse has alighted upon my shoulder' assures him of the requisite solitude for creativity and reverie.

THE LOTHARIO

There is never an easy way of informing a friend that his wife is sleeping with another man. Derived from the Italian 'Cornuto' gesture, this sign subtly informs him of his woeful predicament without ever mentioning that it is you who is her new paramour.

THE DIVERSIONARY

One of the most commonly used of hand signals, the 'may I have the bill please?' gesture should be accomplished with an arabesque flourish. It has the effect of sending the waiter scurrying, leaving you ample time to vacate the premises without paying.

THE AVARISTIC

Parties are often spoilt by bores droning on about escalating house prices. This tedious oaf at least has the decency to demonstrate the monthly accrual of his house value in hand signals, thus sparing fellow guests of smugness dressed up as genial conversation.

THE ASSERTIVE

Curtailing the wrong-headed ramblings of fools and knaves requires clear and unequivocal evasive action. The 'Speak to my hand' gambit is sometimes the only way of silencing the slack-jawed mewlings of sports enthusiasts and educationalists.

THE DROUGHT-STRICKEN

With filthy coffee emporia cropping up on every street corner, the 'Good Heavens, it's time for a nice cup of tea' signal equips an Englishman to withstand the homogenising effects of global capitalism, and to strike a blow for individuality and freedom.

THE DOUBLE BLINKER

This enigmatic gesture, the origins of which are lost in the mists of time, seemingly possesses an almost universal currency. A rough translation might be, "Sir, my admiration for your charming young daughter knows no bounds."

THE SENIOR MAN

This jovial cove confidently uses the 'Obey me' command to assert his natural authority over others. A famous naval victory in 1785 has equipped his family with all the skills they need for sensitive and compassionate leadership of hoi polloi.

THE VULGARIAN

Only a scoundrel would employ the hand signal for 'how much does that cost' outside the confines of the Moroccan bazaar or the Parisian bordello. A man of style either steals what he needs, accrues massive debts or pays exhorbitant bills without quibble.

THE INTELLECTUAL

Shy academics can sometimes find it difficult to articulate ideas verbally. This boffin utilises a complex juxtaposition of finger manoeuvres and a commonly found bathroom toy to explain the main tenets of Kantian dialectics to a room full of enthralled party guests.

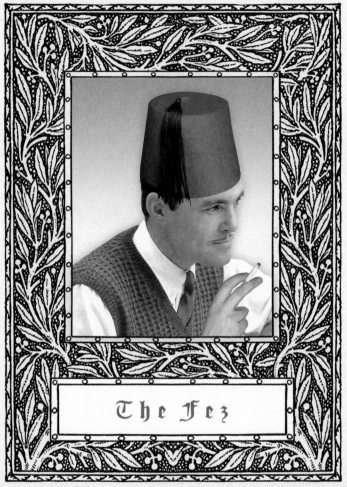

The Fez

One of the hats acceptable for indoor usage, the Fez may be worn comfortably whilst reclining on a chaise longue dreaming of foreign lands. Soaring away on a flight of fancy is far more appealing to a gentleman than actual physical travel. This chap's jaunty headgear, coupled with a pungent hasheesh and the attentions of his Bedouin boy servant, provides him with a one-way ticket to Elysium.

Calmer Sutra

𝔗𝔥𝔢 𝔞𝔫𝔠𝔦𝔢𝔫𝔱 𝔞𝔯𝔱 𝔬𝔣 𝔞𝔠𝔥𝔦𝔢𝔟𝔦𝔫𝔤 𝔰𝔢𝔵𝔲𝔞𝔩 𝔠𝔬𝔫𝔤𝔯𝔢𝔰𝔰 𝔴𝔦𝔱𝔥𝔬𝔲𝔱 𝔞𝔫𝔶 𝔠𝔬𝔫𝔧𝔲𝔤𝔞𝔩 𝔲𝔫𝔭𝔩𝔢𝔞𝔰𝔞𝔫𝔱𝔫𝔢𝔰𝔰

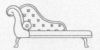

𝔗wo centuries ago, during the reign of Queen Victoria, sexual repression reached such a puritanical frenzy that nobody in polite society dared to make love at all. Conjugal unpleasantness, as the sexual act was known, became strictly the preserve of prostitutes, morphine addicts and the poor. Wealthy aristocrats, realising that their class would die out if they were not propagated, adopted a new form of sexual activity known as the Calmer Sutra, devised by Dr Theodore Wimpole of the Royal Society of Gynaecology and Gymnastics. The Calmer Sutra demonstrated a series of sexual positions that allowed married couples to achieve the desired results of copulation without recourse to nudity, unpleasantness or petting. The Calmer Sutra was published in 1848 with 50 easy-to-follow diagrams illustrating the different positions. We have reprinted an extract from the first edition with six of the original illustrations.

LIFTING THE BRIM

This position is appropriate for the courting couple. It is simple for the novice to master, requiring the gentleman to incline his torso slightly towards the lady, gripping the brim of his hat and raising this object to a height of approximately six inches. The lady should place her left hand upon her breast, whilst leaving her other hand free at her side. The gentleman may note a slight stiffening in the fingers of the lady's right hand, which will serve to indicate that conclusion has been reached.

The Reading Of The Letter

The beauty of this position is that the gentleman and the lady are not required to be in the same location as each other. Each

should compose a letter to the other, restricting its content to sensible subjects such as family matters, descriptions of flowers etc. The letter should be read while seated on the edge of an ordinary upright chair, in a well-ventilated study accompanied by a chaperone. The elbows are to remain firmly placed upon the table during the reading, in order to prevent the unacceptable vice of onanism.

The Explanation Of Things

This position is only suitable for married couples in the privacy of their nuptial homes. The gentleman should stand alongside an armchair, adopting an oratorical stance. The lady places her right hand on the back of the armchair, bowing her head and listening attentively. With his left hand on his hip, the gentleman begins to explain something complicated to the lady, such as how the Royal Mail functions. The act may be prolonged by the lady asking the gentleman some questions when he has finished speaking. The conclusion is reached when the lady finally grasps what the devil her husband is talking about.

The Roar Of The Lion

This is also for the married couple and should not be attempted until the above position has been mastered. A friend or sister of the wifelet may be invited to join in, thus forming a species of *ménage a trois*. The two ladies must install themselves upon the chaise longue, while the gentleman stands at a 45 degree angle to the starboard of the chaise, with his left hand holding the backrest. With his right hand raised for emphasis, the gentleman roars and rages about things that displease him; this may be anything from the lowering of hemlines to the raising of taxes. The ladies are to adopt a distraught air, breaking into uncontrollable fits of sobbing when the gentleman reaches his conclusion.

The Swoon

The ladies can be highly entertained by gentlemen who are able to perform amusing tricks, such as swooning at will. During a chaperoned walk in the countryside, the gentleman should suddenly drop to the ground near a pleasant thicket. He should remain entirely unconscious while the lady hovers over him adopting a mien of extreme agitation. At this point, smelling salts are to be gently used to revive the gentleman. The addition of the chemical compound *anylum nitratus* to the salts can have a highly stimulating effect on the conclusion.

THE TAKING OF THE BISHOP

The game of chess is an extremely rewarding experience for the happily married couple to share. The gentleman should be seated upon a straight-backed chair for the duration of the game (which can often last for several hours). The lady should remain on foot before the table, with one hand upon the edge of the board for support. The reason for the gentleman remaining seated is that he is to play the entire game against himself. The ladies are mentally unequipped for the complexities of chess and their role therefore is simply one of observation. The achievement of checkmate, signalling conclusion of the act, is indubitably a highly satisfying moment for both partners, especially after a five- or six-hour game.

Cornucopia

The reaper of fruits, he represents gluttony and overindulgence
and as a result is permanently in debt

Etiquette for Infants

September is the time of year when the fruits of our loins tend to make their appearance, having been sown during the bleak and bitter months of winter. It is all very well to pop a little infant into this cruel world of ours, leaving it to fumble its way through the vicissitudes that life will inevitably toss into its path, but with a little help a child can be given that edge over his peers. Some early grounding in etiquette and one-upmanship can make the difference between the carefree life of the *flâneur* and a dreary adulthood composed entirely of board meetings and sales conferences.

Here are some pointers for the under-fives, to help them understand the ways of the world and allow them to carve an insouciant furrow through the muddy meadows of human existence.

ENTERTAINING AT HOME

Being more or less bed-ridden and very pleasantly immobile, most of a young infant's entertaining will be done in the homestead. The child's entourage of attendants, special dietary requirements, large plastic toys, bedding and replacement undergarments also make him a complicated and risky item to shift about too much.

When you are receiving at home, try to unblock any unpleasant liquids from the throat and stomach before the guests arrive. An adult will not take kindly to you if he has to spend the entire meal with an epaulette of your vomit on the shoulder of his hacking jacket. The general rule with vomiting is, if something you've been fed *doesn't feel quite right*, then throw it up immediately.

Ask for your high chair to be placed at the head of the table, if possible. You will find it difficult to keep up with the big people's conversation, so you'll have recourse to a lot of dribbling, spoon dropping and food throwing to get their attention.

DINING OUT

Sometimes the big people have difficulty in finding a babysitter and will be forced to take

you with them on a dinner engagement. Be aware that nobody will want you to be there, so you will have to make that extra special effort to make your presence felt.

Upon arrival, ingratiate yourself with one of the staff by slipping them a small gratuity (pinched from your mother's handbag). The willing servant will then oblige you with regular shots of malt whisky or Armagnac into your milk bottle. Getting help with gaspers can be more difficult. You'll have to get your confidante to slip you away from the adults on some pretext. Getting him to show you the horses is a good one. Once you've reached the stables, simply hide in a corner behind a gee-gee and puff away while Jeeves keeps lookout.

BABYSITTERS

Being left alone in the house with a charming young lady in her mid-teens for the entire evening is one of the high points of infancy. By the time you reach 16, your thoughts will be exclusively devoted to the pursuit of this activity, so enjoy it while you can. The young lady will be slightly ill at ease the first time she sits for you, so try to reassure her as soon as she arrives. While she's being introduced to you and shown the provisions and audio-visuals, give her a sly wink, as if to say, "My, they're a boring lot aren't they? At least we young folk understand each other."

Once the big people have left the house, give her a few minutes to settle in before establishing contact. You've probably been put in your cot while she languishes in the living room, and this situation has got to be changed. A polite whimper, gradually increasing in urgency, should persuade her to bring you in to sit with her. Once you are ensconced on the sofa, vomiting or pooing are strictly no-nos. These are not courting habits you want to cultivate and take with you into your teens.

MEETING FELLOW INFANTS

With regards to your peers, there are quite simply two groups: those in the know and those in the don't-know. Keep your attentions firmly fixed on the former and you should go far in later life. The in-the-knows are the short trousers who have access to secret supplies of liquor and tobacco and a network of links with servants across the borough. The others are the sort of fellows who grow up into stupefyingly dull bank clerks who report people for fare dodging.

How are you to recognise each type, when you're all swathed in terry towelling and blankets and look more or less the same? Simple. The ones who start bawling in the presence of other babies are not worthy of your time. If there are several infants present, say at a birthday party, the correct response to any red-faced tantrums is to turn obliquely on your side and study the wall with composed fascination. This will gain the respect and admiration of right-minded little folk.

The Glory of Debt

As a general rule, the good character of any man may be judged by the size of the debts that he amasses throughout the course of his lifetime. An advanced state of indebtedness will obviously mark any fellow out as an attractive sybarite and a chap worthy of reverence and praise. On the other hand, a chump who leaves his affairs 'in order' (as the phrase goes) obviously possesses a frugality and meanness of temperament that is as perverse as it is unforgivable.

With these truisms in mind, we were delighted to discover the existence in the United States of America of a cult dedicated to the glory of debt. Although some readers may be inclined to believe that North America is not necessarily the natural home of Chappish behaviour, it just goes to show that even in a country plagued by concepts as wrong-headed as fast food, leisure wear, canine costumiers, dental perfectionism and 'drive thru' crematoria, there can still be a small glimmer of hope in the all-pervading darkness.

The Cult of Aye Oh Yoo was founded in 1989 under the auspices of Manhattan Svengali, Owen Schedlowdz, in a disused peanut butter factory in the Lower East Side. Disenchanted by the ruthless greed and vulgarity of a modern society, Schedlowdz set to

*Fig. 1. (Above) Owen Schedlowdz as he appears on the increasingly popular 'Never Never Bond',
also known as 'the financial suicide note'.*
Fig. 2. (Right) The race track: a sure-fire way of compiling an impressive portfolio of gambling debts.

work developing a philosophy calculated to 'subvert the forces of global capitalism and promote individual harmony through the accruing of unfeasibly large debts'. Aye Oh Yoo is described as a 'financial suicide cult' by its charismatic leader and he goes on to state that 'only by following a course of reckless borrowing, frenzied buying and hopelessly ill-judged investments, can one hope to reach the ultimate goal of Never Never Nirvana.'

It goes without saying that our American cousins go about things in a startlingly different way to our own good selves, but surely as long as long-term goals are commensurate with the immutable spirit of Chappism, then who are we to judge? On this side of the pond, a debt not built up by dint of face-to-face contact, trust and immense personal charm is quite frankly not worth the paper it's written on. In the US reliance on such new-fangled inventions as the 'credit card' is widespread and is accepted as a necessary evil in the furtherance of noble aims. ('Credit where credit is due' is one of their mantras.) The embracing of 'plastic' enables acolytes to build up their credit portfolios in novel ways. One of these is harnessing modern jiggery-pokery such as the so-called 'World Wide Web'. Although it remains something of a mystery to right-minded fellows in Britain, apparently it is possible to access 'sites' dedicated to such reassuringly terrestrial concepts as casinos, bookmakers, antiquarian bookshops and purveyors of all sorts of gentlemanly requisites. Due to the vast size of America and the huge array of credit cards on offer, it is possible to acquire quite mind-boggling debts before one's name is blacklisted and all cards are revoked. After this, cult members must fall back on more traditional methods of credit.

Apart from the Internet room (the use of which is rigorously monitored) the old custard factory (now renamed The Grand Temple of Higher Purchase) runs many different workshops covering various disciplines that a cult member is expected to master. These include classes in the following.

1. Confidence Building – Pupils are taught how to instill others with confidence. Ensuring that bookies, bank managers, tailors, relatives, etc, really do believe they have every chance of being repaid is the first rung on the ladder to an impressive portfolio of credit.

Fig. 3. A cult member attempts to obtain a non-secured loan for his 'client' (in actual fact, a frighteningly realistic dummy) by using a combination of well-developed ventriloquism skills, forged identity papers and immense personal charm. On this occasion the bank manager eventually granted a generous loan of $3000.

2. Networking – We are all judged by the company which we keep. Cult members are encouraged to insinuate themselves into polite society at every turn. Dallying about town with exiled aristocracy or playing baccarat with the Maldavian ambassador is calculated to gain one the respect of all and sundry, nurture the fiction that one is a man of means and send one's credit rating soaring.

3. The Cultivation of Expensive Tastes – The quality of a debt is as important, if not more so, than its quantity. A $2500 debt built up over time engaging the top class services of a good tailor or buying *objets d'art* at a local auction house is a far more impressive accolade than $25,000 chalked up purchasing soft furnishings over the World Wide Web. Cult members are instructed that they must 'look for a higher purchase', and that 'God is in the retail'.

4. Creativity – Special admiration is reserved for the invention of novel methods of gaining credit. Figure 3 illustrates one such tactic. Figure 1 shows another invented by Owen Schedlowdz himself. Issuing his own currency of Never Never Bonds, Owen hopes that the very attractiveness of its design will gradually lead to it being accepted as legal tender in the Lower East Side.

5. Forgery – Although cult members are encouraged to build up debts legitimately in the first instance, there comes a time when most of one's options are curtailed by one's name becoming 'mud' amongst most financial institutions. The only option at this point is to ply one's craft further afield or indulge in a little forgery, creating false documents, passports, etc, that can secure a whole new 'credit personality'.

6. Squander – The gaming table and the racetrack have always been stylish and efficient methods of losing vast amounts of money in a very short time. Novices are introduced to the basic tenets of placing wagers on the horses (Fig. 2) and casino craft.

7. Costly Love – A refreshing alternative to the sickly hippy ideal of 'free love'. Showering a lady friend with expensive trinkets, taking her for a romantic meal at Jean Georges, followed by a box at the opera and rounded off by a night of passion at the Waldorf Astoria should be enough to send your credit provider into paroxysms of panic. Students are also trained in the art of high-risk liaisons such as having an affair with the under-age daughter of the local police chief or a dubious *amourette* with a transsexual lap dancer from the Bronx. Such trysts can only end in financial disaster, either through an ensuing costly court case or blackmail.

This is where the mastery of Owen Schedlowdz's code of ethics comes to bear. A novice to the creditential arts may at this point observe that a fellow might soon find himself banged up in the local penitentiary. But as Schedlowdz swiftly confirms, 'doing time is regarded as one of the greatest accolades that can be bestowed upon a debtor'. Here a

chap can while away the days, in the confident knowledge that without lifting a finger he is chalking up significant costs at the expense of the rate payer. Rather than paying his debts to society, he is in actual fact tricking society into incurring more debts on his behalf. Cult members are trained to serve their prison sentences without quibble, maintaining sanity through a system of meditation. Sitting cross-legged on his bunk as the call for lights out echoes about the concrete walls and the bestial howls of fellow inmates fade into the night, a cult member will constantly repeat the low guttural mantra of higher purchase:

"Ayeeeeee Oooooooh Yoooooo ...
Ayeeeeee Oooooooh Yoooooo ...

Fig. 4. Prison should never be regarded as a punishment but, rather, an ideal opportunity to incur more debts at the expense of the public purse.

The Meerschaum

 Ah, season of mists and mellow fruitfulness. This ludicrous buffoon sports a huge and elaborately carved meerschaum in an attempt to emulate the ancient 'horn of plenty' and thus distract attention from his obvious deficit in the physical stature department. Accepting his limitations and adopting a modest briar would be far more likely to secure the respect of his colleagues, family and friends.

Transgressive Education

Education, education, education – so good they named it thrice' goes the old ditty, and indeed it is difficult to overestimate the importance we should attach to the guiding, nurturing and fine-tuning of the intellects of our youth. Sadly, the teaching of children is a sacred trust that has been somewhat neglected in recent years by a sickly bunch of miscreants who refer to themselves as 'educationalists'. (There is surely no group in today's society more deserving of our utter contempt.) Since the 60s, the influence of the Nuffield Foundation, a wrong-headed coterie of trendy professors, has actively peddled the derisible falsity that students should be instilled with a passion for learning (or 'learnacy', as the current buzz-word has it) through kindness and the application of 'hands on' practical work in the classroom. For some unknown reason, the age-old tradition of coercing youngsters to acquire knowledge by beating sense into them with the aid of a large knobbly stick has, for the time being, been abandoned, and what a pretty pass we have come to as a result.

Thankfully, there are still a few sane individuals about today who are willing to stand up and be counted and offer our callow youth a brighter future. Among these is Sir Vincent Clowdesley-Shovel, redoubtable polymath and man of leering, who has been for many years developing some of the most efficacious and far-seeing techniques that can be employed in the moulding of formative minds. The Clowdesley-Shovel Academy for Young Gentlemen has been up and running for barely four years now, but it is already producing some quite breathtaking educational results.

Sir Vincent realises that in order to imprint proper modes of conduct on his young wards he must first rid them of the baggage that may have been drummed into them by former schools and conventionally thinking parents. Rendering a student a blank sheet, a

palimpsest, is a lengthy business involving a copious amount of random flogging, sleep deprivation and casual roughings up, but in his heart of hearts he knows he is doing his boys a tremendous kindness. A kindness that in the fullness of time, after an extensive remedial course of physiotherapy, they will no doubt readily thank him for.

When this preparatory period is completed, a whole new world of opportunity and delight awaits the pupil. Orthodox assumptions about curricular structure are thrown out of the window and the jolly adventure of 'transgressive' education may begin.

CONVENTIONAL MORES

The premise of conventional education seems to be the production of 'useful members of society'. Sir Vincent would find it hard to imagine anything worse. He is implacably opposed to a system

Fig. 1. Enthralled sixth form students soak up the subtleties of speciality Swedish arthouse cinema.

that regards youngsters as faceless office fodder, pitiful gerbils on the treadmill of capitalism, programmed to prop up the status quo of mindless ambition and corporate greed. Instead of stock Pavlovian behaviour, standing up or sitting down at the ring of a bell, the Academy hopes to produce a generation of interesting, entertaining and psychologically intricate (if not a little disturbed) individuals, drunk on the opportunities that life might deal them. To these ends he has made sure that timetables are tolerably designed to fit in with a gentleman's sleep patterns. The day commences at 12.30pm with individual *sartorials*, short discussion periods designed to advise students on the cut and style of their clothing. The following classes are pleasantly punctuated at 3pm by afternoon tea and (as long as everyone can be bothered) continue through the afternoon until around 6. Instead of the insolent clang of a school bell, the end of the students' travails is announced by the serving of a round of expertly prepared dry martinis and hot buttered crumpets adorned with lashings of Patum Peperium.

SCIENTIFIC ENQUIRY

Finely attuned to the overall ethos of the Academy, Mr Cunningham, the head of the science department, has designed a syllabus not only calculated to inform his students of

recent development in the fields of biology, chemistry and physics, but also to make men out of boys.

One example of his novel approach to teaching is his organisation of the annual cross country race. Although the Academy looks disapprovingly upon any form of physical exercise, the yearly race is tolerated as a valuable teaching aid in the field of post-Darwinian theory, which reappraises the true significance of the famous phrase 'survival of the fittest'. In order to drive his point home, Mr Cunningham takes pot shots at the front-runners of the race with his trusty flintlock shotgun in the hope of instilling his wards with acceptable modes of civilised behaviour (Fig. 2). After all, a boy who willingly runs around in circles on a cold autumn day clad only in his underwear for no better reason than the desire to be 'first' could hardly be regarded as 'fit' for anything. Students soon learn that abandoning the idiocy of sport and skulking in the shrubbery, drawing heavily on high-tar cigarettes is a far safer and more respectable pastime for a young man on the threshhold of life.

In chemistry class, students are particularly advanced in practical work in the laboratory (Fig. 3). Emphasis is placed not only on understanding the principles of chemical reactions,

Fig. 2. Mr Cunningham prepares to demonstrate the harsh realities of post-Darwinian evolutionary theory to the lower-sixth cross-country team.

but also the everyday usage of their products. Students set their own agenda and are required to outline their findings in a thesis at the end of the year. Recent topics have included, 'Lysergic Acid Diethylamide: Chemical Journeys into the Infinite' and 'Nasal Rapture: An Olfactory Analysis of Frangipani, Sandalwood and Bergamot'.

THE LIBERAL ARTS

Nowhere is Sir Vincent's radical agenda more apparent than in the area of the arts. To keep students on their toes, he decides on the timetable literally minutes before entering the classroom, usually by random word association aided by the fortuitous spinning of an empty wine bottle. Comfortably ensconced in a roomy armchair, he will elucidate the topic of the day. Some of his more celebrated discourses are the stuff of school

Fig. 3. A chemistry student carefully isolates useful compounds for later internal usage.

legend. Classics such as: Cufflink Appreciation; New Departures in Antimacassar Design; Narcissism for Beginners; A Brief History of Teatime; Reclining Decorously; The Basics of Pipe Smoking Technique; Charming Things to Say to the Ladies; and Insincerity with a Smile, are still talked about with relish by his eager pupils.

A recent innovation that has proved especially popular with the students is the introduction of the sixth form cinema club. Thanks to the sterling generosity of one of the parents, film director Mattias Groebel of Amsterdam, the school now boasts unlimited and free access to some of the major releases of speciality Swedish and Dutch arthouse cinema (some of which actually star Mr Groebel's wife, Sonia). One glimpse at the intense concentration on faces of students in the darkened lecture hall bears testament to the educational benefits of early exposure to the challenges of the avant-garde (Fig. 1).

So it seems that at least in one small sector of our educational establishment proper and true values are again being taught. Those parents wishing to enlist their offspring for the Clowdesley-Shovel Academy will be delighted to learn that admission is free, the school is self-supporting, the tutorial costs and upkeep of the establishment being entirely funded by the sale of products currently being produced by the chemistry department.

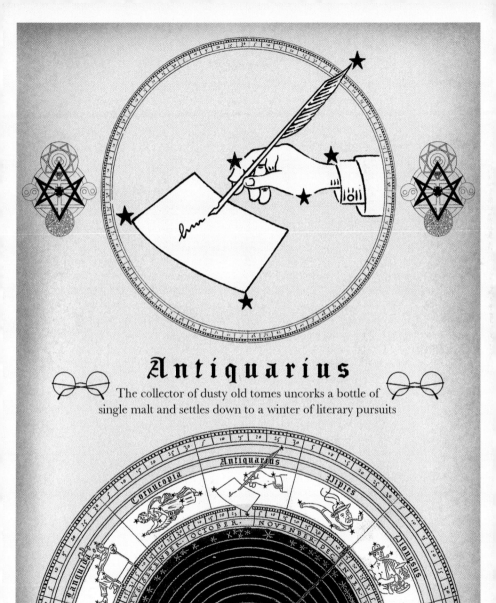

Antiquarius

The collector of dusty old tomes uncorks a bottle of
single malt and settles down to a winter of literary pursuits

12th October 1492… Christopher Columbus landed on the coast of Cuba,
becoming the first European to set foot in the New World.

Grave New World

The recent discovery of a logbook belonging to Professor Sherwood Filibuster of Edinburgh caused startling revelations among the Chappist community. It had been previously assumed that certain regions of the world remained entirely unchartered by gentlemen, but Filibuster's logbook clearly shows that a Chappist expedition to the New World had been successfully achieved in 2002. Here is a reproduction of the original logbook from that legendary voyage, when a small group of gentlemen explorers set off to discover what lay beyond the unchartered territories to the northwest of Watford.

18th October 2002. I write this journal in the second-class carriage of a motionless railway wagon standing somewhere between Watford and Tring. The journey from London Euston to Milton Keynes Central should ordinarily be completed within 45 minutes, but severe delays to the service have resulted in numerous periods of inactivity such as this. I shall therefore take this opportunity to introduce the other members of our expedition. Professor Marmaduke Saunders is a lecturer in zoology at the University of Warwick. His interest in the anthropology of Buckinghamshire was the subject of a recent paper entitled *Some Observations on a Series of Tring Skulls*. The third member of the team is Mr Edgebaston Mountforce, a noted archaeologist with a particular interest in regions densely composed of concrete. We are also accompanied by three able porters whom we found loitering around Euston station. They initially expressed reservations about undertaking this voyage, many of them claiming that relatives who had gone to Milton Keynes were never seen again. However, a few cans of extra strong lager soon assuaged their fears.

ARRIVAL

As we exited from Milton Keynes Central station, it was evident that the surrounding land had been intensely cultivated. As far as the eye could see, there stretched vast tracts of concrete and asphalt, dotted hither and thither by monoliths of steel and glass. Saunders and myself agreed to head our party in the direction of the densest area of concrete, presuming that if there were any natives here, they would have constructed their dwelling in such an area.

After some 20 minutes on foot, somewhat delayed by the continual complaints from the porters about their load (three armchairs, one gramophone player, a cocktail cabinet, navigation instruments, two month's supply of claret, an upright piano, a tea service and a set of encyclopaedias), we arrived at what appeared to be the entrance to a walled

settlement. Various hieroglyphs adorned the sides of the gates, which Mountforce claimed to resemble some glyphs he had seen during a recent expedition to the Americas. We plunged through the tall glass doors into a vast concrete vaulted arena. The first impression was one of complete sterility. Not a stick was out of place in this enormous tiled atrium, whose borders were composed of glass vitrines displaying the local handicrafts, which we took to be market stalls.

The natives were of great interest to Professor Saunders. At first he limited himself to studying them from a distance for the purposes of classification. Their physiognomy resembled the inhabitants of many British cities, but with somewhat pasty and bloated faces and the eyes a little dull and listless. Their costume was not unlike that of their distant cousins, the Kingstonians: a species of nylon two-piece overall with markings along the sleeve and on the breast. Their feet were clad in footwear of some synthetic fibre, bearing a singular mark which we were to come across later at the entrance to their temple.

BASE CAMP

At this juncture we decided to set up camp. With the hour of luncheon approaching, we instructed the porters to light a fire in a clearing between a market stall bearing the hieroglyph 'GAP' and another marked 'STARBUCKS', where we proposed to roast a suckling pig we had brought with us. While taking our aperitif, we observed the eating habits of the Miltonians.

Their diet is predominantly carnivorous and is eaten from brightly coloured paper bags. They prefer not to eat at table, but while walking around or standing before many of the vitrines around their settlement. Their food has a rather unpleasant odour and they seem to derive little enjoyment from it. A number of the natives were intrigued by our roast suckling pig, approaching our table gingerly while we dined. Yet when we offered them a small portion with a glass of claret, they shyly retreated and replaced their noses in the paper bags containing their food. Instead of wine, the natives drink a curious sweet beverage from tall plastic beakers. Mountforce and I sampled some from a discarded beaker and found it to be a noxious substance such as one would use to clean the silver.

HERE BE FRIESIANS

After luncheon, we agreed to press on towards the interior of the settlement. The only flora we encountered were some tall palms growing from concrete enclosures lining the thoroughfares of the settlement. Professor Saunders took some samples of the earth around them, much to the amusement of the natives. The Miltonians seemed a friendly enough bunch, if a little dull-witted; our attempts to engage them in conversation were not entirely successful. Those that consented to speak to us did so in a curious polysynthetic dialect which Professor Saunders was unable to classify with any certainty. He was, however, able to communicate fairly effectively with the natives by utilising a blend of Wolverton and Tring dialects.

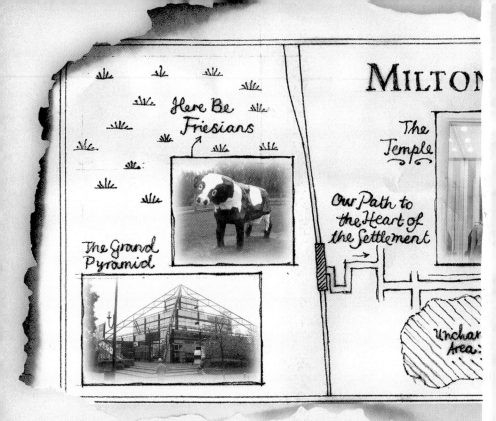

Here Be Friesians

The Temple

Our Path to the Heart of the Settlement

The Grand Pyramid

MILTON

Uncharted Area

The question we were most eager to ask was, "Where are your cows?" During our preparatory research in the map room at the Carlton Club, many rumours had reached us concerning the existence in Milton Keynes of some concrete cows. The mystery surrounding their origins had infused our quest with a quality taking it beyond the realms of mere science. Yet the Miltonians themselves seemed unable to offer a satisfactory response. We decided to postpone our search for the cows until after we had penetrated to the heart of the settlement.

I wanted to purchase a little trinket for my wife as a souvenir of my visit to Milton Keynes. Most of the market stalls were selling examples of the local costume, but at prices no cheaper than London. I attempted to barter with one of the stallholders for a cashmere sweater, only to be ushered out of the place by a large burly fellow in a dark uniform and hat. So far this had been the only indication of hostility from the Miltonians, and it raised the question as to whether they experienced familiar urban problems such as crime and delinquency.

There seemed to be no evidence of any criminal activity, but as we ventured deeper into

KEYNES

Totem Pole.

Natives feeding at the Lake.

the settlement we saw several examples of what we took to be penal colonies. Behind large glass panels completely open to public view, men and women were shackled to complicated torture instruments, where they were forced to run on the spot by aggressive guards. Others, clearly in great pain, were trapped beneath enormous weights and pulleys, engaged in a futile effort to remove them.

TOWARDS THE TEMPLE

This was evidently a society that on the surface seemed pleasant and unthreatening, yet was clearly controlled by stringent measures of law and order. We were intrigued as to whether the Miltonians practised any form of religion, and after several more hours of negotiating our way through the labyrinthine corridors, we found what we took to be the inner sanctum of the settlement.

This was a small aperture in the wall, large enough for one or two souls to pass through at a time. Above the entrance was the mark we had witnessed upon the natives' footwear.

It was clear that this particular building, although in appearance much like all the others, held great importance to the Miltonians. Watching the entrance from a safe distance, we observed one native respectfully wolfing down his fodder outside the shop and wiping his hands on his trousers before entering the temple. Those who came out of this tabernacle seemed elated in some mystical way, many of them clutching large plastic bags. They had evidently purchased vestments from the temple, presumably for them to wear during worship at home, and this prospect appeared to excite them very much indeed.

BUT WHERE BE FRIESIANS?

Now that we had seen the epicentre of the Miltonian settlement, we were further intrigued by the nature of the concrete cows. Were they the relic of some distant Miltonian pagan culture, since replaced by the worship of the marked vestments? We left Mountforce at the table of a restaurant named 'Burger King' to execute some detailed drawings of the surrounding architecture, and I set off with Saunders and one of the porters towards the outskirts of the settlement.

Our enquiries finally yielded some information about the cows, from a kindly old woman at a bus stop. She informed us that they could be reached upon the number two omnibus, which just happened to be departing. Upon the bus, we pressed the old woman for more detail about the origin of the cows, but our questions only alarmed her. We alighted at the spot she indicated, finding ourselves upon a deserted stretch of motorway.

We rained curses upon the old woman, who had clearly duped us into getting lost in revenge for our inquisitiveness. However, we took the opportunity to explore the terrain surrounding the settlement of Milton Keynes.

Although heavily forested, the hand of man was in strong evidence in this manicured woodland. Concrete paths cut through the grassland, with the trees placed at intervals too geometric for Mother Nature; even the very grass under our feet exuded an air of inauthenticity. We were beginning to feel disheartened by our discoveries when, suddenly, through a clump of trees, we saw the cows.

There were six of these beasts, crudely carved from concrete and painted with black and white markings. They were arranged in a pattern resembling that of a stone circle – I wished Mountforce had been there to offer an explanation. Professor Saunders did offer a hypothesis that the ancient Miltonians, in worshipping the cow, may have shared the beliefs of the Hindus, but I was reluctant to concur. If this were the case, why would their diet consist mainly of beef patties in bread?

We took some photographs of these singular concrete animals for the benefit of Mountforce's research, and made our way back to the settlement to find him. Once we had packed our equipment, we began our journey towards the railway station, arriving just in time to catch the 18.54 to Euston. We could hardly wait to return to the Carlton Club and report our findings, for deep in our hearts I believe we all knew that many of the great archaeological textbooks would have to be rewritten as a result of our discoveries in the New World.

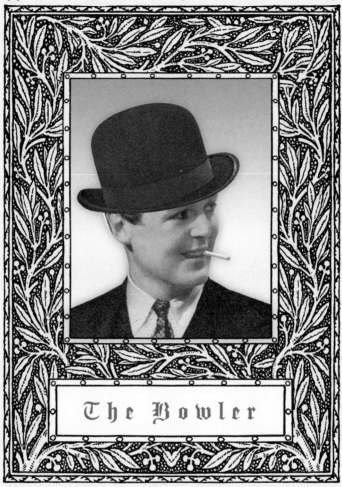

The Bowler

 Unapologetically old-fashioned, the Bowler has had a long and unfortunate association with the unsavoury practices of gainful employment and religious extremism. Happily, it is currently enjoying a rehabilitation in musty reading rooms across the land as the only piece of headwear sturdy enough to retain the contents of a brain brimming over with tempestuous romanticism and abstruse literary knowledge.

Seasonal Vegetable Sculpting

There is a disposition on the other side of the Atlantic that regards the sculpting of vegetable matter as a particularly poignant way of celebrating the festival of Allhallows Eve. Traditionally, a pumpkin has been used for such purposes, but an adventurous Chap (perhaps inspired by sterling examples of vegetable sculpting, that can sometimes be found on the tabletop during a visit to a chinese restaurant) may be seized with the urge to experiment. Here are number of carving suggests for a fellow to while away the lengthening hours of the October evenings.

1. Pumpkin Heads – Instead of carving the face of a brute with a beastly grimace, attempt a schematic representation of the quintessential Chap.

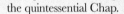

2. Radish Noh Mask – Whittling away at a radish is a surefire way of impressing the ladies. Watch the fillies gape in wonderment as your nimble fingers convert this diminutive veg into a miniature Japanese Noh mask.

3. Parsnip Pipe – This conveniently shaped root vegtable provides the perfect raw material for the creation of smoking implements. The natural flavour and moisture of the parsnip will ensure the smoothest of smokes.

4. Potato Taj Mahal – Strictly for the advanced vegetable sculptor. Spend the autumnal evenings at home carving a large King Edward into a scale replica of Shah Jahan's world-famous mausoleum. Attempting to emulate the intricate fretwork and delicate finials of the original will keep you absorbed for hours.

5. Carrot Flannels – A humorously shaped, bifurcated carrot is an ideal vegetable item for fashioning an attractive model of a crisply creased pair of grey flannel trousers.

Do It, Youssef!

As the new moon waxes on the night of October 27th, so begins Ramadan, the period of fasting occupying the ninth month of the Moslem calendar. It is during this time that, as men of principle and sound moral fibre, we should show extra consideration for our Bedouin houseboys. Since no food, drink or cigarette smoke is permitted to pass the lips of every good Moslem between the hours of dawn and dusk, the poor little fellows are likely to be at their most fragile and irritable. This is the ideal time to set your houseboy some stimulating tasks around the house, in order to keep his mind off those mounting hunger pangs and nicotine cravings.

The concept of Do-It-Yourself is naturally anathema to any right-thinking fellow. If, furthermore, he has managed to acquire a suitable houseboy, then this little Bedouin will be equally horrified at the prospect of putting on a pair of overalls and bending over a Black and Decker Workmate. The ideal houseboy – let us call him Youssef – is a languid sort whose expertise lies in the preparation of sumptuous hookahs and excellent cocktails. He should also be able to perform amusing little dances, be a first-class poker player and able to acquit himself in several foreign tongues. The price you often have to pay for these charming qualities is laziness, dishonesty and a tendency to disappear for days at a time.

So let us imagine a typical morning for Youssef during Ramadan. The day might begin with his tackling some of the annual domestic chores, such as emptying the ashtray, doing the washing up and changing the bed linen. These may seem fairly straightforward, but bear in mind that the intoxicating odour wafting from the dining room as you breakfast on devilled kidneys and kedgeree will severely put little Youssef's faith to the test.

By midday, when Youssef has completed the first of his tasks, it might be wise to ensure his continued enthusiasm by allowing him to do something he finds enjoyable, such as mixing you your first dry martini of the day. Bear in mind that the little blighter will also waver when exposed to the forbidden fumes of gin and vermouth; we all know that Ramadan is the only time when Youssef bothers to observe his religion's prohibition of alcohol.

Youssef is now ready to move on to grander tasks. Instruct him to devote the afternoon to retouching your fresco of The Rape of the

Sabines in the smoking room. Years of pipe tobacco, opium fumes and cigarette smoke can take their toll on your average fresco, especially when you insisted on it being painted only with original materials, such as egg-tempura, iron oxide and ground lapis lazuli. Unfortunately, you might now find a coating of brown grime over the figures of Romulus and the Sabines. You could assist Youssef by projecting a slide of the original Poussin on to the ceiling, using the elliptical method of camera obscura trompe l'oeil projection, while Youssef scampers among the rafters on a stepladder with an oil painting set. With your expert assistance, it shouldn't take him more than a few days to retouch the expressions of terror on the faces of the Sabines.

Youssef deserves a suitable reward after this mammoth task. Ramadan rules permit him to break his fast after sundown, so get him to prepare a delicious repast for the two of you, and devote the rest of the evening to feeding Youssef with grapes and fondant fancies before a roaring fire.

You may want to give Youssef a relatively simple task for the day after his backbreaking work on the fresco: building an extension to your pipe rack, for instance, or constructing a bill-shredder. Get him to take an ordinary desktop printer and replace the print heads with

some rusty nails and drawing pins. Then simply place a telephone or gas bill in the paper slot, switch it on and watch £243.96 reduced to a pile of unrecognisable shreds. If you find the sight of bills too distressing, get Youssef to make a bill shield decorated with a pretty William Morris design to place on top of the printer.

Youssef will now be ready to tackle your largest DIY project: converting your garden shed into a Turkish bath. The first stage of construction will involve constructing a masseurs' entrance at the back of the shed, plus a changing room for them. A pit must be dug in the centre of the shed floor, into which a stone enclosure for the hot coals can be placed. Various elegant walkways, seats, massage tables and pools can be constructed out of marble, surrounded by pleasant mosaics depicting lavish Ottoman scenes. The exterior of the shed will have to be fully soundproofed to prevent the emission of moans and groans from the interior.

When Ramadan ends on November 26th, you can reward Youssef by allowing him to test the temperature of the completed Turkish bath, as well as trying out each of the four Turkish masseurs you will employ. After his month of hard graft on an empty stomach, Youssef will be more than happy to report on which of the four burly Turks gives the most delicate effleurage.

Pipies

The avid smoker of briar, Churchwarden and meerschaum
sinks joyfully into his armchair with a large tub of navy shag

Pipe Signalling

𝔑 o fellow of quality or worth would ever countenance being seen in public without some instrument of tobacco consumption. Whilst snuff and cigarettes are compact, subtle and convenient ways of keeping one's nicotine levels up to scratch, and cigars and pipes such as the meerschaum and calabash are apt to get one noticed, when it comes to perfection of design the implement of preference always has to be the trusty briar. Sleek and harmonious, a straight briar fits conveniently into any suit pocket and when in use greatly enhances the beauty of a gentleman's physiognomy by forming, as it does, a *golden section* in ratio to the axis of the nose.

Considering the importance of the briar to a Chap's everyday existence, it should come as no surprise that this ubiquitous piece of hardware is currently being adapted by today's young gents into a light-weight and eminently practical signalling mechanism. Using principles gleaned from other codes such as semaphore, Morse code and North American Comanche smoke signals, pipe signalling has slowly evolved in environments, such as the race track, cocktail parties and formal business meetings, where rapidly escalating

How d'you do

Absolutely charmed to meet you again

Would you care for a drink?

Do you have a penchant for arthouse cinema?

My needs are strong, urgent and unnatural

Charming filly to your starboard bow

Mine's a large Talisker sans glace

Lady Caroline is looking rather stunning this evening

background noise levels or the necessity of confidentiality make non-verbal communication a must.

Novices should be aware that it will take some time to become fully *au fait* with the intricacies of pipe signalling. Successfully manoeuvring the pipe stem between the teeth takes quite a bit of tongue and muscle control and the blowing of successful smoke rings can sometimes take months to master, but with daily practice the speed of message transmission will gradually increase.

Once the basic skills have been learned, pipe signalling gives the smoker recourse to a rich, multi-layered and expressive language, which he will often ask himself how he ever did without in the first place. (Some examples of commonly used phrases can be seen below.)

From its utilitarian origins, the language of the pipe has now developed to a point where some adventurous souls are now using it to give vent to artistic self-expression. A good example of this can be seen at the weekly meetings of the West Huddersfield Avant-Garde Poetry Circle. A special section has been put aside for poems created entirely for the medium of pipe signalling. It can hardly do justice to attempt a translation of such a poem into the written word, but here, for the curious reader, we have attempted an approximate text equivalent of Kenneth Prout's delicate *Haiku for a Pipe*, a moving study of bereavment and loss.

> *Glowing bowl of wood*
> *Extinguish the burning leaf*
> *Pleasure is no more.*

I'm a trifle down in the dumps

Sir, your trouser creases do you the utmost credit

Let's not beat about the bush here

£3500 – take it or leave it

Fifteen to one in the 3.45 at Epsom

Please leave me to my personal reveries

Can't say I think much of the vol-au-vents

I say, I seem to have run out of tobacco

1st November... Day of the Dead in Mexico, when the souls of departed family members and ancestors are remembered.

L'Amour De La Mort

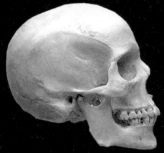

))) **estern society has** a long way to go when it comes to facing up to mortality and recognising the mute proximity of the grim reaper. Those who dare to broach the subject during a dinner party or show a healthy interest in the intricacies of embalming (perhaps by softly kneeding the dearly departed's facial tissue at a family funeral) are rebuked for being morbid or somehow a little odd. In the developing world, and especially in Mexico, no such taboo exists (the annual Dia de los Muertos is a firm family favourite), but this does not necessarily mean that a determined Chap enamoured by the ceremony, ritual and absurd mystery of this 'last journey' has need to travel thousands of miles in order to encounter a pleasing array of artefacts and locations related to death to keep him amused during the month of November. There are plenty of charming locations across Europe that are capable of slaking the thirst of even the most assiduous necrophile.

From the humblest village graveyard, to the great mausoleum at Halicarnassus. From the dank inconsequential demise of a household pet, to the wholly unexpected evisceration of an much-loved relative in a freak holiday accident, the angel of death is a constant companion on our journey through life. Surely, each one of us, faced with the incontrovertible fact of our own mortality, can react in only one of three ways.

1. Hysteria and blind panic – Leading to indigestion, insanity, bored friends and large laundry bills.

Fig. 1.

2. Ignorance and denial – Leading to an excessive dependency on interior furnishings, shopping, vitamin tablets, cosmetic surgery, Disneyland and golf.

3. Acceptance, embracement and ritualisation – Leading to vigour of the mind, art, literature, philosophy, cigarettes, vintage port and chafing.

On balance, it seems clear that number three is the only option that comes close to cutting the mustard for the recreational requirements of the decadent gentleman. So take up your finest ebony cane, drench yourself in frankincense, and let us take you on a brief journey in search of sepulchral pulchritude.

First stop will be Kensal Green Cemetery in west London, the first of the capital's great Victorian necropolises. Wafting down the gravel paths, it is the mausolea, statuary and epitaphs that exude flamboyance, defiance or intemperance from beyond the grave that hold our interest. Andrew Dacrow, the circus impresario, is commemorated by a richly vulgar monument of a Graeco-Egyptian bent, complete with sphinxes, beehives and angels. No embellishment is resisted, no cliched metaphor remains unexplored. John St John Long slumbers beneath a recriminating diatribe against the detractors of his medical cure. Despite deaths of patients and legal proceedings, Long promoted his elixir unabated, only to refuse to take it himself on his own death bed. The simple headstone of the wholly admirable Kerry Richard Deering (1953–1984) reads, "He burnt the candle at both ends. But oh what a lovely light."

Inside the Anglican Chapel there is a velvet-covered catafalque of not inconsiderable charm. This hydraulically operated marvel of the age would descend slowly through the floor at the conclusion of Victorian funerals. It strikes one as being an eminently suitable resting place for the chiffon-clad Catherine Deneuve, shrouded in lilies, in the highly singular necrophiliac scene of Bunuel's 1967 classic, *Belle de Jour*.

But onward and forward. We must whisk you away to our second port of call. The Eternal

City beckons. There lies in the eastern quarter of Rome, in the crypt of the church of Santa Maria della Concezione, a series of chambers of such a bizarre integrity that one immediately senses that some continental jiggery-pockery is afoot. This is the Cimitero dei Cappuccini, the final resting place of several thousand Capuchin monks exhumed, once thoroughly decomposed (due to limited grave space), and their bones converted rather touchingly into a variety of ceiling roses, rococco friezes, cornices and morbid tableaux. (Fig. 1). It occurs to us that there could hardly be a better way of commemorating a life well lived than converting one's mortal remains into an attractive architrave, pediment or dado rail. In the final room, a diminutive child's skeleton, that of a Barberini princess, emerges from the ceiling, appearing to swoop, like some forlorn wingless bird over the viewers below.

And so to Paris. The French, in death, as in their lavatorial arrangements, tend to leave very little to the imagination. Few places exhibit the bare-faced morbid cheekiness of the Paris catacombs. These old abandoned quarries were converted in 1786 as a solution to the overcrowding of Parisian graveyards, especially the Cimitiere des Innocents. Millions of bones were cleared from the old charnel houses and stacked in the claustrophobic corridors. As we enter the ossuary, we are greeted by the cheery legend, "Arrete! C'est ici L'Empire de la Morte." The pulse quickens, a breath taken and thence forth on both sides we are flanked by dimly lit piles, six feet tall and two feet deep of human skulls and bones. Although we are much affected by the spectacle, we are forced to conclude that such an overcrowded and frankly communal approach to interrment would be quite unsuitable to a man of style.

A swift Ricard at a nearby café to wring the damp out of our ligaments and we are off to our final destination and, in many ways, the highlight of this giddy smorgasbord of deathly delights. The Musée Fragonard d'Alfort is rarely included in guides purporting to reveal the treasures of Paris, but it is surely one of her most singular attractions. Housed in the Ecole Nationale Vétérinaire d'Alfort, it contains 18 specimens of the work of the anatomist, Honoré Fragonard, the cousin of the painter, who developed a unique technique for the preservation of flayed cadavers. Despite the production of well over 700 specimens and being made the head of the anatomy department of the Ecole de Santé, his method of preservation is said to have died with him.

The centre piece of the museum has been variously described as 'Le Cavalier' or, alternatively, 'The Winged Horseman of the Apocolypse'. The tableau presented to us consists of a cantering flayed horse being ridden by an equally flayed rider. The 'winged' part of the title refers to the curiously splayed muscles of the man's back which have been extended upwards and outwards to form a leathery fan behind the rider's head. This is sensitively completed by the addition of a pair of ludicrously staring glass eyes and an entourage of dancing foetuses around the horses feet.

Virtually overcome in the presence of such beauty, we are reminded how the proximity of death provokes within us a lust to seize the moment and live life as if we are gods. We therefore retire to a nearby café and seek solace in the mundane certainties of oysters and champagne.

*15th November 1904… King Camp Gillette, of Fond du Lac, Wisconsin,
was granted a patent for the world's first safety razor.*

Dada Depilation

When it comes to base trickery, it seems that Madame Nature is not above playing an absurdist jape or two on her unsuspecting minions. Chief among these is her decision to pepper the human form, to a greater or lesser extent, with hair.

Whilst a luxuriant beard, shag-pile chest growth or hirsute calves are rumoured to be strangely impressive to the ladies, it can still be highly distressing to a young fellow on the threshold of manhood to find his body populated by a sudden influx of ludicrous shrubbery. Never in the right place at the right time, hair can steadfastly refuse to grow on one's cheeks as a young man when precocious masculinity might be calculated to place one ahead of the pack in the *game of love*. Likewise, in later life, when maintaining a look of road-

Fig. 1. The Demi-Huelsenbeck. An example of 'art-depilation' first seen in the Cabaret Voltaire in 1916.

worthiness depends on it, hair often takes it into its mind to emulate the wildebeest of the Serengeti and perform a mass migration from top of the scalp, only to take up permanent residence inside the nostrils, on the earlobes and over the shoulderblades.

It hardly comes as a surprise that for millennia, men and women have devoted a great deal of time and ingenuity attempting to rid themselves of, at least limit the extent of, this unsightly affliction. The Romans explored various techniques of bodily deforestation including the use of dangerous depilatory concoctions, waxing, plucking, abrasion, singeing and shaving. The ancient Britons (according to Julius Caesar) had a convention of shaving all of their body hair except their head and upper lip, and then gaudily painting themselves from head to foot with bright, blue woad. Priests and holymen of many cultures have intentionally sported abjectly foolish haircuts (involving large swathes of shaven scalp) in order to symbolise their transcendental aspirations and their rejection of what we may regard as the everyday accoutrements of a gentleman, such tortoiseshell combs, brilliantine and pomade. And ladies and gentlemen of the 18th century brought

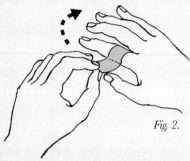

Fig. 2.

depilation to new aesthetic heights by shaving off their eyebrows and replacing them with press-on mouseskin substitutes. These had the advantage of being perfectly shaped, various in colour and repositionable for maximum dramatic effect.

So, contrary to appearances, the spiteful nature of hair and our attempts to tame it should be regarded not as a burden or a threat, but, instead, a singular opportunity for creativity, sensuality, sublimity and rebellion. Dadaist depilation allows you to do just that.

And so, the wheel comes full circle. History urges us to revitalise this noble and ancient craft. In its purest form, dadaist depilation should be pointless, cynical, desperate and utterly random, but in the real world, where bourgeois society has instilled within us an urge to justify our actions, you may feel that you need one or two pointers as to why you should wish to indulge in such a practice in the first place. These reasons number two, and two only.

1. Pure rebellion – designed to promote social incohesian and to undermine the very fabric of society.

2. Sensual pleasure and profound self-indulgence.

You might wish to commence your programme of hair removal with some simple and subtle forays, which will be discernable to no one but yourself. In an oppressive workplace environment, for example, you can harness the depilatory qualities of common or garden adhesive tape to mitigate the boredom of endless hours of paid employment. Firmly apply the tape to the back of your fingers, one at a time, as shown in Figure 2, and then remove with one swift flick of the wrist. The fine hairs will come away with a satisfying sting. Ouch!

A similar principle may be applied to the hairs of the lower leg region. Whilst sitting at your 'work-station', reach down and wrap a length of tape around your ankle, just above the sock line. By this stage you may wish to graduate onto brown parcel tape, the superior quality of adhesive used on this product will remove all but the most recalcitrant of hairs. Having denuded both legs up to knee level, the chances are you'll be lusting to continue with your programme of experimentation. It's probably time to purchase a Sheffield steel shaving requisite or proprietary brand of depilatory cream. Try turning up to the office one morning wearing only one sideburn or trim one side of your military moustache into a thin pencil. Randomly lop off parts of your coiffure and act as if you are completely unaware of the fact.

Surely, now would be a good time to revive the 18th century practice of eyebrow removal. Why not visit your local furrier and get him to knock you up a pair of immaculate animal hide replacements? Mouse is very good for everyday wear, but the use of angora, cashmere or leopard skin should not be ruled out. Use you're intuition and judgement as

Fig. 3. Depilation using a stencil. This young cove displays sterling creativity by selectively depilating his chest hair to produce a stunning likeness of Dada poet, Tristan Tzara.

to where to place them. Half way up the forehead will endow you with hauteur and gravitas. Abandoning yourself to asymmetry will give you the general demeanour of screen idol Roger Moore. For an extra avant-garde *frisson*, advanced eyebrowers may even consider placing their brows on the underside of the eye rather than above.

As the rank absurdity of your appearance increases, you will no longer feel able to venture out of your rooms into the wider world. This is all to the good. You will lose your job due to non-attendance, and confined to the squalid environs of your rented accommodation you will be forced to contemplate the great issues of the day, such as the aesthetics of contemporary pyjama design or the metaphysical resonances of daytime television.

Dedicate the winter months to furthering your breadth and scope of your quest. Use stencils and depilatory creams in ways that God never intended. Etch likenesses of literary figures such as Baudelaire or Barbey D'Aurevilly into your chest hair or fashion a miniature portrait of the Marquis de Sade in the dank recesses of your upper thigh region (Fig. 3).

Before retiring into seclusion, make sure you stock up on a few sturdy rolls of masking tape. These can be used to form impromptu and free-form templates when dealing with the removal of hair from the scalp. Some stunning results may be obtained through spontaneous acts of creativity. Refer to Figure 4 for some guidance on the most effective method of applying tape stencils.

When you finally find that 98% of your body surface is all-but defoliated, your mind may turn to those particularly torrid, equatorial regions of the human anatomy that dare not speak their name. It is not for *The Chap* to dictate how you approach such difficult and sensitive territories, but, suffice to say, cheap titillation and sordid rudery should play no part in our journey of self-discovery.

Do as you may and as you see fit, but when the burgeoning buds of spring sprout forth, so too should you allow your follicles to give birth once more. The season of closeted introspection is over. Next winter we will do the same, but for now, walk onto the street a proud man, give vent to manly hirsutetude and embrace the shaggy bestiality of destiny.

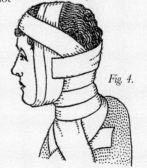

Fig. 4.

Who Dares Trims

The Story of the Special Hair Service

ℐn 1941, at the height of World War II, the British Army began to notice an alarming number of its men returning from the front looking rather unkempt. Tidy toothbrush moustaches had become huge unruly handlebars, smooth billiard-ball chins were peppered with bristles and, in some cases, whole beards had sprouted forth, leaving their victims barely recognisable. These unfortunate men were naturally kept out of action for several days while a skilled barber attended to them, and thus many valuable battle hours were wasted.

In response to this mounting crisis, Brigadier Dudley Puddingbowl-Shearer came up with the idea of a special task force of skilled barbers. This highly trained regiment would be skilled in all forms of hairdressing, as well as stealth tactics and maximum-conflict survival skills. They would be dropped directly behind enemy lines to deal with any hirsute crises in the heat of battle. They would be called the Special Hair Service.

The Special Hair Service (SHS) were trained to 'style hair with extreme prejudice'; their task was to gain access to the fighting force and see to their follicular needs without any interruption to the military campaign. Ideally, the recipients of the services of the SHS needn't even know they were there at all; not until a soldier returned to base camp or glanced in the wing mirror of a tank would he realise that he had been given a splendid short-back-and-sides or a moustache trim. Another role that the SHS played was to rescue soldiers who had been taken hostage behind enemy lines and forced to grow beards to render them unrecognisable. To this day, the rumour is maintained that one battalion of the SHS was being trained for a campaign to kidnap Adolf Hitler's famous 'Hitler' moustache at the height of the Blitz, to deflate enemy morale.

Some of the most highly respected and worshipped heroes of World War II came out of the SHS. Norman 'Scissors' Clark was a legend for his skills in tidying up a floppy fringe in a matter of seconds. He once managed to trim the moustaches of an entire battalion of the Highland Light Infantry while they launched a night-ambush on some German paratroopers. Charlie 'Cut-Throat' Wilkinson was said to be able to shave a corporal at 17 paces, and Rodney 'Tweezers' Hamilton could always be relied upon to quickly deforest the ears of a radio operator.

Initial training takes place at Shearer Hairlines in Hereford, the SHS's UK base, where recruits perfect their hostage-shaving skills in a long, windowless building with a row of barber's chairs, known as the 'Cutting House'. The weapons used in the Cutting House are precision hairdressing scissors and Wilkinson cutthroat razors, on practice targets made from old wigs and balloons covered in shaving soap. SHS recruits also have to ascertain where they are most needed; they are trained to distinguish sounds at night, for example, the sound of bristles chafing the starched collar of a uniform, or breathing restricted by a bushy moustache.

Certain hairdressing skills are developed to an extraordinary level of ability in the Cutting House. Among these, the use of the safety razor in close-quarter barbering

(CQB) is the most impressive. The object is to teach the soldier to burst into a room occupied by several bearded men and to shave them all in 60 seconds. The recruits also have to learn how to minimise the risk of innocent casualties; on a hijacked aircraft, for example, when a non-combatant bystander might have his perfectly decent pencil moustache shaved off by accident.

At any time, one complete squadron of 11 SHS soldiers is always on instant stand-by at Hereford, shaving gear packed and a memorised codeword in their heads. They are often tested for readiness at unsocial hours. A few years ago the codeword 'Sweeney Todd' filtered among the customers of the Hare & Hounds in Hereford. Many of the local drunkards thought it was an amusing word game, but 11 men gave each other the nod, quietly drained their glasses and made their way to Shearer Hairlines. "This time it's for real, lads," they were told when they arrived, "We're going to Colombia." (Some British diplomats had been kidnapped and were being held behind Enemy Hairlines in Cali.)

The role of the SHS commando has changed very much over the years. No longer are we besieged by Fritz and his tidy blonde partings and comedy moustaches. Today's enemy is the wearer of intimidating beards of quite formidable proportions. Charlie 'Cut-Throat' Wilkinson, in charge of the 1942 plot to steal Hitler's moustache, now 92 years old, had this to say on the matter: "I'd certainly have my work cut out for me if I had to do the equivalent mission today. You'd need a pair of shears just to make a dent in some of the beards those towel-heads wear."

One thing is certain: even the most elusive enemy, once tracked down by the SHS, will not be stroking his beard and muttering sinister incantations for long. He is far more likely to be mournfully rubbing a billiard-ball chin and crying into his Kalashnikov.

Dionysus

The devotee of wine and its more sinister derivatives
plunders his wine cellar of its entire contents

8th December 1869… Leopold von Sacher-Masoch signed a contract in which he agreed to be the slave of Fanny von Pistor for a period of six months.

New Directions in Flagellation

The intriguing hobby of flagellation (self or otherwise) may be regarded by some as a slightly outré way of passing the dull afternoons of midwinter, but it is pastime that should not be discounted out of hand by a gentleman open to a little sensual experimentation. From obscure saints and religious zealots to Scandinavian health fiends, from the 19th century suprasensualists to the 20th century Conservative MP, the fashion for thrashing oneself or one's friends with a variety of implements seems to have rarely waned in popularity.

At the transcendental end of the market, 'mortification of the flesh' has long been regarded as just the ticket for holy men wishing to tap into a spot of spiritual ecstasy. In this respect, scourging oneself with a length of knotty rope cannot be bettered. Girolamo Savanorola, the 15th century Dominican monk, beat himself silly in the bijou austerity of his Florentine monastic cell, and at certain times of the year Islamic youths greatly enjoy lashing themselves with bladed scourges (a procedure that may seem a trifle over the top to the untrained Western eye).

Fig. 1.

In Scandinavian countries, a different approach is employed. In scenes of unparalleled depravity, naked men beat each other with bundles of birch twigs in order to stimulate health and circulation. Such an unabashed and 'healthy' attitude to flagellation may be very well and good inside the confines of a Swedish sauna, but is hardly a method that should be emulated by an Englishman.

For a template more suited to the sensibilities of today's decadent gentleman, we should turn to the very singular practices of Leopold von Sacher-Masoch. In

Fig. 2.

his famous novel, *Venus in Furs*, he details his sterling adventures in suprasensual excess, or 'being beaten senseless by his lady friend' as it is more commonly known. Although being duffed up by one's paramour is not an essential component of flagellation, it is Sacher-Masoch's decorum, philosophising and willingness to experiment that should act as an inspiration to the modern gent.

Naturally, any procedure that involves the shedding of blood or the removal of too many items of clothing is tasteless in the extreme and tantamount to rudery, but by moderately thrashing oneself or others whilst wearing reassuringly well-tailored clothing, a fellow can take his dignified voyage into the abstruse realm of the senses. Cat-o'-nine-tails, scourges, flails, riding crops and bullwhips have always had their place in a gentleman's recreational repertoire, and experiencing the sharp bite of the lash through a sturdy layer of 20oz plain worsted can be immensely invigorating. But as with all things, a fellow's tastes can become rapidly jaded by repetition and there will come a time when the boundaries must be pushed further in order to keep one step ahead of encroaching ennui.

Instead of sticking to the predictable repertoire of instruments, a creative Chap should be willing to innovate in order to keep himself, his lady friend and his chums entertained. For instance, rewarding one's spouse at the end of a long day with a light trouncing using a commonly found household implement, such as an attractively designed carpet beater (Fig. 1) or egg whisk (Fig. 3) is calculated to secure you at the centre of her affections as firmly as the sun holds sway over the heavenly orbits. A spirited young lady will be more than happy to return the favour by coming at you with a loaded vacuum cleaner bag or a power cord from the electric kettle. The resultant collection of welts should be regarded as a true measure of the depth of her love for you.

But it is on days when you find yourself alone and abandoned by the Muse that a spot of self-flagellation really comes into its own. Rekindle fond memories of that long hot summer in Dar es Salaam by donning a loose Arabic robe and flailing at your back with a ceremonial horse-hair fly whisk (Fig. 2). The madcap adventures

Fig. 3.

Fig. 4.

and jolly scrapes you got into with your Tanzanian chums will soon come flooding back in a wave of uncontrollable nostalgia.

Another way for a fellow to reach down into the well of his being and bring to the surface a brimming pail of lost emotions is the liberal usage of a delicate instrument known as the 'cravat o' two tails' (Fig. 4). This stylish flail is constructed from a pure silk paisley cravat firmly attached to a woven leather handle. Wearing a sheer and lovely white poplin shirt, allow the merest tip of the cravat to flicker suggestively about your midriff whilst reciting some particularly beautiful lines from Samuel Taylor Coleridge's drug-fuelled ramblings.

For the outdoor type or those who pride themselves on an earthiness of personality, a more rustic stance may be taken. Whilst on a fishing expedition this gnarled old country-man (Fig. 5) takes the opportunity to indulge in some dual-action spanking using a couple of freshly caught salmon. It allows him to commune with nature in the most uncompromising fashion and simultaneously give praise to the river nymphs for their bounty. This manoeuvre should on no account be attempted whilst wearing anything other than a heavy-weight Irish thornproof tweed. Residual fish oils will serve to weatherproof such clothing, but may prove ruinous to suits constructed of the less robust materials designed for indoor wear. Meeting the Duchess of Montmorency in a dinner jacket reeking of old mackerel, for example, is not calculated to win favour and will do nothing for your social standing with the smart set of Fitzrovia. ❦

Fig. 5.

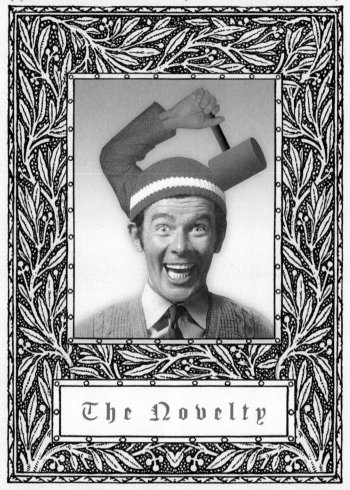

The Novelty

 The seasonal horror known as the 'office party' often leads to staff bolstering their self-esteem through an immoderate use of alcohol. A man, devoid of spontaneous wit or sparkling conversation, may drunkenly try to compensate for his shortcomings by wearing eyecatching headwear of dubious provenance. This simpering nincompoop fondly imagines that he is 'entertaining' and 'fun to be with'. He is not.

The Semiotics of Drinking

'**In vino veritas**' wrote Pliny the Elder (no doubt inspired by a hastily dispatched bottle of retsina). And who could possibly deny alcohol's starring role when it comes to getting to grips with the eternal verities of the human condition?

Striding manfully into any place of adult refreshment, one only needs an ounce or two of perspicacity and the eyes in one's head to read the truth of people's lives merely through the way that they drink. In order to spare readers the chore of researching the subject themselves, we have spent many gruelling months of laborious field work on your behalf, propping up bars in highly disreputable venues, chatting to ladies of questionable virtue and quaffing stunning quantities of virulent liquor. Our suffering is your gain.

We humbly offer you the fruits of our labour.

THE CONNOISSEUR

This ridiculous looking fellow might know a thing or two about vintages and chocolatey aromas, but appearing too finickity and fastidious has never been, and never will be, calculated to win the hearts of ladies. Expertise is often the mask of impotence.

THE SUBLIME

The man who throws his life and soul open to malt whisky, undiluted and sans glace, is a man of rare distinction and impeccable character. More a religious vocation than a drink, ancient malt ordains its imbiber as the heir to Dionysus's sacred mantle.

THE VULGARIAN

This demented guttersnipe obviously thinks that he is hip and with-it to drink foreign lager straight out of the bottle. Such an assumption is as sickening as it is wrong-headed. He richly deserves a good thrashing and a savage kick in the billingsgate.

THE PLAINLY RIDICULOUS

"Sir, there seems to be an extraneous object in the neck of my bottle. Kindly remove it at once." This imported affectation leaves a right-minded fellow irate and perplexed, and is merely designed to disguise the lamentable taste of the lager within.

THE REAL ALE MAN

There is no shame for a man of sensibility and sophistication to indulge, on occasions, in an honest pint or twelve. By imbibing malty brews and guffawing loudly, this fellow gains the common touch, and, thus, the respect and trust of hoi polloi.

THE ARRIVISTE

A glass filled with a lurid concoction, piled high with fruit and novelty items singles this man out as a social inferior who imagines that distinction and *cachet* can be bought by the ounce. His profession in sales is wholly incompatible with being a gentleman.

THE SERIOUS DRINKER

A slight overdependence on the stimulating effects of gin are not a worrying matter, but more a sign of generosity of spirit and a robust and forthright approach to life. This fellow's highly admirable behaviour makes him a prince among men.

THE SENIOR MAN

To the civilised man about town, indecision as to what to drink should never present a problem. At all times of the day the noble martini can be regarded as a haven in a fickle and turbulent world. Sexual gratification at this man's hands is virtually guaranteed.

THE UNDER-AGED

Sometimes it can be difficult for a publican or owner of an off-licence to spot an under-age drinker attempting to flout the law. This young turk dupes his adversaries by the fiendish ruse of donning a frighteningly convincing facial appendage.

THE SUBLIME

It is a tradition among artists and so-called 'creative' people to imbibe eccentric drinks such as Absinthe, Thunderbird and Creosote. Despite ceaseless mythologising about the dangers of such beverages, there is no evidence of long-term harm.

26th December… St Stephen's Day, or Boxing Day, when money was collected in alms-boxes in churches and distributed to the poor after Christmas.

Christmas Devilment

Throughout history, festivals designed to mark the advent of the winter solstice on the 21st December could hardly be described as thin on the ground. Nordic Yule festivals, Roman Saturnalia and Sol Invictus celebrations, and Druidical Alban Arthan come to mind as but-a-few of the outlandish divertissements on offer. It is widely acknowledged that the early Christian church commandeered such celebrations as a convenient juncture to commemorate the birth of Christ, but no matter whether your sympathies lie with paganism or Christianity, one thing is certain, the midwinter festivities have now been sequestered once again, and this time by the vulgar and unscrupulous powers of commercialism.

Yuletide is now nothing more than an opportunity for large corporations to tout their wares in an extended orgy of salesmanship that lasts from late October to precisely 5.30pm on the 24th of December. By this point, consumers are judged to have fulfilled their economic destinies, and families, whipped up into a frenzy of unrealistic expectation and prefabricated sentiment, are cut adrift and left to their own devices. Is it any wonder that, having been sold the myth of the perfect Christmas, disillusioned family members, confronted by the mind-numbing horror of reality, then spend the following days venting their frustrations on each other, and rekindling age-old resentments and feuds?

You may erroneously see it as your role to act as peacemaker in such circumstances and seek to build bridges and spread concord, but on reflection a wise cove will realise that

Fig. 1.

there is very little point attempting to save souls that have already offered themselves up for slavery. In actual fact, the only way that the modern Christmas can be made more bearable is to remain aloof, and instead of being drawn in to the hostilities, harness the skirmishes and general nastiness as an elaborate war game. Much amusement may be gained by artificially inducing internecine conflict.

We have already seen how Beelzebub can prove an invaluable ally when it comes to office management (see page 52), but allowing oneself to be guided by the quiet voice on your left shoulder can also provide a number of jolly ruses for making the Christmas holiday a great deal more enjoyable. If the Devil has the best tunes, then why not get your relatives to dance to them? Base your tactics around the Roman festival of Saturnalia. The name Saturn is derived from *satus* (meaning sowing). Try coming up with ways of 'sowing' the seeds of discontent and conflict amongst your nearest and dearest. Indeed, instead of celebrating Saturnalia in its original guise, give serious thought to throwing yourself headlong into the fray, going the whole hog and renaming the day as Satanalia.

Greet the Satanalian morn by tampering with the contents of Christmas crackers. Start the party off with a swing by replacing dreary mottos and weak jokes with pieces of paper either with the general observation, 'We are all the servants of Lucifer', or a spot of well-planned mendacity such as, 'It was cousin Darren who stole Uncle Edward's pocket watch in 1998'. At the same time, place the watch (which you half-inched yourself in a moment of boredom and subsequently discovered to be less valuable than you had first thought) into another of the crackers in place of the plastic novelty. The resultant confusion and bickering will prove immensely satisfying and will goad you on to greater feats of ingenuity.

As a variation on this theme, try swapping over name labels on presents under the Christmas tree. Sit back with satisfaction as Great-Aunt Mildred receives a Marylin Manson CD, whilst dangerously maladjusted Darren finds himself the proud owner of a daintily crochetted lavatory roll cosy (Fig. 1).

The morning round of hostilities will have barely settled down when the next stage of the day can be entered into. Many families across Britain will look forward at three o'clock to Her Majesty's Address to the Commonwealth. Great-Aunt Mildred will be particularly looking forward to this as the highlight of her day. It would be a shame to ruin it, but ruin it you must. With the bile of Mephistopheles running around your veins you could do no other. All good things come to those who wait, and if you have been wise you will have recorded last year's Queen's speech on a video tape and will have spent the last 12 months seeking advice on how to dub a new sound track over the original. Surreptitiously insert the doctored tape into the video player and play it in place of this year's address. Hearing Her Majesty recommend the sterling benefits of amphetamines or intoning incantations in the low sibilant whisper of the possessed will provide the perfect opportunity for lively discussion and debate.

As Christmas Day wears on, the advanced tedium can lead to someone suggesting a dreaded round of party games. Dusty cardboard boxes will be produced from under beds, and strange plastic toys and faded boards will be laid out on table tops. Fortunately, most board games can be enlivened by attaching a gambling element to them. A hefty wager on a game of Mousetrap or Trivial Pursuit will render them far more bearable. Of course, upping the stakes a little by suggesting that the forfeit for loss should be a human life will add some much needed edge. Figure 2 illustrates a game of Russian Kerplunk. The addition of a revolver loaded with a single bullet is a sure-fire way of injecting excitement into a jaded and predictable Yuletide staple. Spinning the cartridge and pulling the trigger every time a marble is dislodged is guaranteed to make the party go with a bang.

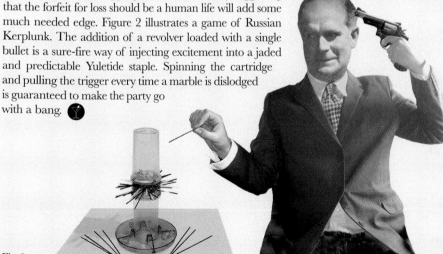

Fig. 2.

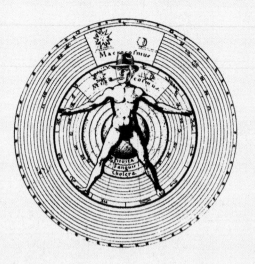

Messrs Temple & Darkwood gratefully acknowledge the following chumrades in the distillation of this Almanac.

Robert Baker

Meg Davis

Matthew de Abaitua

Robin Harvie

Tony Lyons

Tony McSweeney

Andy Miller

Fiona Salter

Susan Smith

Toby Welfare